WERE YOU THERE

When They Crucified Our Lord?

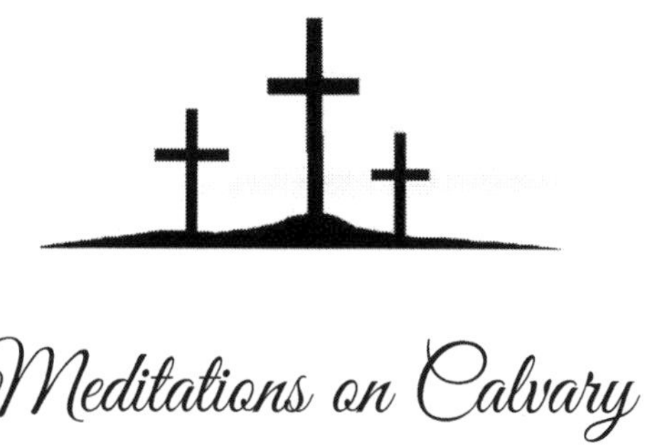

Meditations on Calvary

LINDA BONNEY OLIN

Were You There When They Crucified Our Lord?
Meditations on Calvary

Cover and interior designs by Linda Bonney Olin

Published by Linda Bonney Olin, New York, USA
www.LindaBonneyOlin.com

ISBN-13: 978-0-9911865-3-2
ISBN-10: 0991186532

CONTENTS

PREFACE

"Were you there when they crucified my Lord?"

The haunting words of this African-American spiritual inspired me to delve into the Bible for details of Jesus Christ's arrest and execution. Who was there? What did they see, and hear, and feel? What did they do?

The meditations, songs, and discussion questions in this book will read between the lines of scripture. We'll explore the events of that day through the eyes of people who were there (or were conspicuously absent) when they crucified our Lord. Drawing closer to the cross for a deeper understanding of what happened on Calvary, we seek to draw closer to Jesus.

Were You There When They Crucified Our Lord? Meditations on Calvary originated as a weekly Lenten soup-and-study presentation for my local churches. That's a great way to use it, but the material lends itself to individual devotional reading and small group study as well.

Scripture verses are quoted from several different translations. Other translations and Bible study tools can be found online at BibleGateway.com.

Each chapter includes at least one musical meditation. The songs are generally set to existing tunes that are quite easy to sing. Two songs ("My God, Why" and the round version of "Where Were the Twelve") are more challenging; simpler alternates are provided for those. Songs in this book also are suitable to be used separately in worship services.

Visit the Audio page at www.LindaBonneyOlin.com to hear Emrys Tyler's moving renditions of "Who Is This Man" and "Jesus, Please Remember Me," recorded during the maiden voyage of this Bible study at the Harpursville United Methodist Church and Nineveh Presbyterian Church. Other helpful resources for this study and music will be posted on the web site, too.

If you enjoy *Were You There When They Crucified Our Lord? Meditations on Calvary,* please pass the word to other readers. The few minutes it takes to post a review on Amazon—just a sentence or two saying what you liked about the book—would be a huge help. Thank you!

—Linda Bonney Olin

He humbled himself
and became obedient to the point of death—
even death on a cross.

PHILIPPIANS 2:8 (NRSV)

STUDY

1

THE AUTHORITIES

Opening Prayer

Savior Jesus, we shy away from horrifying images of suffering and injustice. But you draw us closer to you, to the scene of your crucifixion. As we look through the eyes of people who were there, witnessing or even causing your pain, never let us lose sight of the fact that it was love that brought you there—love so great that you laid down your life for your friends. Open our hearts to your presence and our minds to the lessons you want us to learn. Amen.

Song

"Were You There" (p. 62; all sing)

- When they crucified my Lord?
- When the sun refused to shine?
- When they pierced him in the side?

Meditation

Our opening song asks, "Were you there when they crucified my Lord?" Each chapter of this study will focus on individuals or groups who were there—and on a few who were conspicuous by their absence.

First: Where is the "there" we're talking about?

The Bible records that Jesus Christ was crucified on a hill called Place of the Skull, which is *Golgotha* in the Aramaic language and *Calvary* in Latin. Both names, Golgotha and Calvary, are commonly used.

The hill was located near the city of Jerusalem, in the present-day nation of Israel. Two thousand years ago, during Jesus' lifetime, that territory was called Judea. It was controlled by the mighty Roman Empire. The Jews who lived there hated and feared their harsh Roman rulers.

But Jewish leaders in Jerusalem hated and feared Jesus of Nazareth even more. His teachings challenged their religious authority. Word began to spread that Jesus was the Messiah, the one God had promised would come to establish a righteous kingdom. This idea posed a clear threat to their own power over the Jewish people.

When Jesus raised Lazarus from the dead in front of an amazed crowd of Jewish mourners, that was the last straw. The religious authorities decided to rid themselves of Jesus permanently (John 11:38–57).

One of the leaders, a man named Nicodemus, had secretly followed Jesus' teachings (John 3:1–21). Nicodemus urged the others to give Jesus a chance to explain his teachings and activities before judging him (John 7:50–52). But they brushed off his advice and went ahead with their plans to kill Jesus.

The religious authorities couldn't legally put a man to death. So they plotted to have the Romans do it for them. They had Jesus arrested for stirring up a revolt against the Roman emperor. That was sure to get the governor's attention! And, most importantly for their plan to succeed, such a crime was punishable by death.

The story continues in the gospels of Luke and John.

Scripture Reading

Then the entire council took Jesus to Pilate, the Roman governor. They began to state their case: "This man has been leading our people astray by telling them not to pay their taxes to the Roman government and by claiming he is the Messiah, a king."

So Pilate asked him, "Are you the king of the Jews?"

Jesus replied, "You have said it."

Pilate turned to the leading priests and to the crowd and said, "I find nothing wrong with this man!"

Then they became insistent. "But he is causing riots by his teaching wherever he goes—all over Judea, from Galilee to Jerusalem!"

Then Pilate called together the leading priests and other religious leaders, along with the people, and he announced his verdict. "You brought this man to me, accusing him of leading a revolt. I have examined him thoroughly on this point in your presence and find him innocent." Pilate argued with them, because he wanted to release Jesus.

But they kept shouting, "Crucify him! Crucify him!"

For the third time he demanded, "Why? What crime has he committed? I have found no reason to sentence him to death. So I will have him flogged, and then I will release him."

But the mob shouted louder and louder, demanding that Jesus be crucified, and their voices prevailed. So Pilate sentenced Jesus to die as they demanded. (Luke 23:1–5, 13–14, 20–24 NLT)

Finally Pilate handed him over to them to be crucified.

So the soldiers took charge of Jesus. Carrying his own cross, he went out to the Place of the Skull (which in Aramaic is called Golgotha). There they crucified him, and with him two others—one on each side and Jesus in the middle.

Pilate had a notice prepared and fastened to the cross. It read: "Jesus of Nazareth, the King of the Jews." Many of the Jews read this sign, for the place where Jesus was crucified

> was near the city, and the sign was written in Aramaic, Latin and Greek.
>
> The chief priests of the Jews protested to Pilate, "Do not write 'The King of the Jews,' but that this man claimed to be king of the Jews."
>
> Pilate answered, "What I have written, I have written." (John 19:16–22 NIV)

Meditation (cont.)

Pontius Pilate believed that Jesus was innocent of the charges brought against him by the Jewish leaders. Yet he condemned Jesus to die a shameful, agonizing death on the cross in order to pacify the mob.

Why would a powerful man like Pilate do such a cowardly, unjust thing?

Consider his dilemma. Pontius Pilate served as governor of Judea at the pleasure of Tiberius Caesar, the Roman emperor. Caesar expected the governor to keep the peace. If a riot broke out in Jerusalem, especially while thousands of visitors were in the city to celebrate the Passover, Pontius Pilate would have to answer to Caesar. That certainly wouldn't help his ambitions for political advancement. So Pilate let Jesus take the fall.

Was Pontius Pilate there on Calvary when they crucified our Lord? No, not in person. As far as we know, he sentenced Jesus to death and then stayed far away from the gruesome punishments his decree set in motion.

Pilate was represented on Golgotha, however, by the Roman soldiers who carried out his orders. They were very much there, not merely as spectators but as active participants.

Soldiers or centurions (officers who commanded units of about one hundred soldiers) are mentioned in verses scattered throughout the gospels. Let's gather up their story and hear it in the form of a soldier's report about the day Jesus went to the cross.

Song

"Who Is This Man" (p. 66/112; male solo)

Meditation (cont.)

The soldier represented in the song is a composite of various soldiers mentioned in the scriptures. He was a professional soldier, rough and tough. He admits he showed no mercy when the whip and the hammer were in his hand. He had schooled himself to ignore the screaming of his victims and the wailing of onlookers. It was his duty to carry out the sentence, and he did it. He sounds as ruthless as Pontius Pilate himself.

Unlike Pilate, however, the soldier probably had no idea that Jesus was an innocent man who had been railroaded by the authorities. As far as the soldier knew, Jesus was guilty as charged, just like the two notorious robbers who were crucified the same day. Jesus had been given a fair trial in the famous

Roman judicial system and was justly sentenced to be tortured and executed; the soldier had no reason to doubt that. At least not at first.

We don't know what actually went through the minds of all the soldiers who dealt with Jesus that day, but, as our song suggests, at least one soldier's belief in Jesus' guilt may well have been chiseled away, bit by bit, by the strange things he witnessed on Calvary:

- The attitude of forgiveness Jesus showed, even toward the man who was grimly nailing him to a cross
- The repentant thief's declaration that he and the other robber were guilty but Jesus was innocent
- The candid manner in which Jesus addressed the Lord God in prayer
- The stormy skies and quaking earth that marked Jesus' death

What an amazing display of divine power that was! It shook even the hardened centurion into crying out, "Surely this man was the Son of God!"

Discussion

Picture a soldier standing watch over Jesus' tomb that Friday night, silently pondering all the things he had witnessed at Golgotha.

1. How might the soldier have answered the question "Who was— Who *is* this man?"
2. If the same soldier stood guard again on Saturday night and Sunday morning, how do you think he would have answered the same question Sunday afternoon?
3. Has God ever used a display of awesome power or extraordinary tenderness or forgiveness to get your attention? How did that experience affect your thinking? Did it change your behavior?
4. What hard-hearted ways do you have? What do you think it would take to shake you into changing?

Closing Prayer

O God, you know the selfish ambitions that cause us to reject the kingship of Jesus, as the Jewish authorities did, and to better ourselves at the expense of others, as Pontius Pilate did. Like the Roman soldier, we can make wrong assumptions about other people that cause us to treat them harshly. Use your awesome power in our lives to soften those hard spots in our hearts. Open our eyes to the love that is ours in your son, Jesus, in whose name we pray. Amen.

Song

"God Be with You till We Meet Again" (p. 64/107; all sing)

2

THE TWELVE

Opening Prayer

Savior Jesus, you know our human frailties so well! No matter how faithfully we think we love you, we can be swept away from you in a moment of weakness and fear. Teach us lessons about your deep love as we hear what your closest disciples did the day you were crucified. Amen.

Song

"Were You There" (p. 62; all sing)

- When they crucified my Lord?
- When his friends all ran away?
- When they nailed him to the tree?

Scripture Reading

(For this reading, designate three participants to read the parts of JUDAS, PETER, and JOHN. Everyone will read the verses for THE TWELVE together.)

> JUDAS: Judas Iscariot, one of the twelve disciples, went off to the chief priests in order to

betray Jesus to them. They were pleased to hear what he had to say, and promised to give him money. So Judas started looking for a good chance to hand Jesus over to them. (Mark 14:10–11 GNT)

THE TWELVE: [On the night of their last supper] Jesus said to them, "All of you will run away and leave me, for the scripture says, 'God will kill the shepherd, and the sheep will all be scattered.'" (Mark 14:27 GNT)

PETER: Peter answered, "I will never leave you, even though all the rest do!" Jesus said to Peter, "I tell you that before the rooster crows two times tonight, you will say three times that you do not know me." Peter answered even more strongly, "I will never say that, even if I have to die with you!" (Mark 14:29–31 GNT)

THE TWELVE: And all the other disciples said the same thing. (Mark 14:31 GNT)

JOHN: They came to a place called Gethsemane, and Jesus said to his disciples, "Sit here while I pray." He went a little farther on, threw himself on the ground, and prayed that, if possible, he might not have to go through that time of suffering. "Father," he prayed, "my Father! All things are possible for you. Take this cup of suffering away from me. Yet not what I want, but what you want." (Mark 14:32, 35–36 GNT)

PETER: Then he returned and found the three disciples asleep. He said to Peter, "Simon, are you asleep? Weren't you able to stay awake for even one hour?" And he said to them, "Keep watch, and pray that you will not fall into temptation. The spirit is willing, but the flesh is weak." (Mark 14:37–38 GNT)

THE TWELVE: He went away once more and prayed, saying the same words. Then he came back to the disciples and found them asleep; they could not keep their eyes open. And they did not know what to say to him. When he came back the third time, he said to them, "Are you still sleeping and resting? Enough! The hour has come! Look, the Son of Man is now being handed over to the power of sinners. Get up, let us go. Look, here is the man who is betraying me!" (Mark 14:39–42 GNT)

JUDAS: Jesus was still speaking when Judas, one of the twelve disciples, arrived. With him was a crowd armed with swords and clubs and sent by the chief priests, the teachers of the Law, and the elders. The traitor had given the crowd a signal: "The man I kiss is the one you want. Arrest him and take him away under guard." As soon as Judas arrived, he went up to Jesus and said, "Teacher!" and kissed him. (Mark 14:43–45 GNT)

PETER: Simon Peter, who had a sword, drew it and struck the High Priest's slave, cutting off his right ear. The name of the slave was Malchus. Jesus said to Peter, "Put your sword back in its place! Do you think that I will not drink the cup of suffering which my Father has given me?" (John 18:10–11 GNT)

THE TWELVE: The Roman soldiers with their commanding officer and the Jewish guards arrested Jesus and tied him up. (John 18:12)

Then all the disciples left him and ran away. (Mark 14:50 GNT)

JOHN: Then Jesus was taken to the High Priest's house, where all the chief priests, the elders, and the teachers of the Law were gathering. (Mark 14:53)

Simon Peter and another disciple followed Jesus. That other disciple was well known to the High Priest, so he went with Jesus into the courtyard of the High Priest's house, while Peter stayed outside by the gate. Then the other disciple went back out, spoke to the girl at the gate, and brought Peter inside. (John 18:15–16 GNT)

PETER: Peter was still down in the courtyard when one of the High Priest's servant women came by. When she saw Peter warming himself, she looked straight at him and said, "You, too, were with Jesus of Nazareth." But he denied it. "I don't know what you are talking about," he answered, and went out into the passageway. Just then a rooster crowed. The servant woman saw him there and began to repeat to the bystanders, "He is one of them!" But Peter denied it again. A little while later the bystanders accused Peter again, "You can't deny that you are one of them, because you, too, are from Galilee." Then Peter said, "I swear that I am telling the truth! May God punish me if I am not! I do not know the man you are talking about!" Just then a rooster crowed a second time, and Peter remembered how Jesus had said to him, "Before the rooster crows two times, you will say three times that you do not know me." And he broke down and cried. (Mark 14:66–73 GNT)

Pilate went back into the palace and called Jesus. "Are you the king of the Jews?" he asked him. Jesus said, "My kingdom does not belong to this world; if my kingdom belonged to this world, my followers would fight to keep me from being handed over to the Jewish authorities." (John 18:33, 36 GNT)

JUDAS: When Judas, the traitor, learned that Jesus had been condemned, he repented and took back the thirty silver coins to the chief priests and the elders. "I have sinned by betraying an innocent man to death!" he said. "What do we care about that?" they answered. "That is your business!" Judas threw the coins down in the Temple and left; then he went off and hanged himself. (Matthew 27:3–5 GNT)

JOHN: [After Jesus was nailed to the cross] Standing close to Jesus' cross were his mother, his mother's sister, Mary the wife of Clopas, and Mary Magdalene. Jesus saw his mother and the disciple he loved standing there; so he said to his mother, "He is your son." Then he said to the disciple, "She is your mother." From that time the disciple took her to live in his home. (John 19:25–27 GNT)

Meditation

If we took attendance at Calvary, how many names would we check off?

Roll call:

- John? "Present!"
- Simon Peter?
- Judas Iscariot?
- James the son of Zebedee?
- James the son of Alphaeus?
- Andrew?
- Philip?
- Bartholomew?
- Thomas?

- Matthew?
- Thaddaeus?
- Simon the Zealot?

That's right. Of the twelve disciples in Jesus' inner circle, only one, the apostle John, is recorded as being present at the crucifixion of Jesus Christ.

Song

"Where Were the Twelve" (all sing; p. 80 or 82/117)

Meditation (cont.)

The twelve scattered when Jesus was arrested in the garden. Wouldn't you do the same, if you were jolted awake in the dark of night by a mob armed with clubs and swords?

Who can blame the disciples for hiding while Jesus was falsely accused, questioned, tortured, and crucified? With Jesus being convicted of leading a revolt against Caesar, his followers in the alleged revolt were surely in danger of their lives too.

The gospels don't indicate where the disciples went or what they did the rest of that Friday, except Judas, Peter, and John. Let's look closer at those three.

Judas Iscariot was probably the only one of the twelve who had nothing to fear from Jesus' enemies. After all, he had conspired with them to betray Jesus. Yet Judas ended up dead. It wasn't the Romans or the Jewish religious authorities that did him in. It was his own guilty conscience. Judas may have been dead already when Jesus was nailed to the cross.

What about Simon Peter? He was generally considered a leader among the twelve.

- He had been the first disciple to acknowledge, "You are the Son of God" (Matthew 16:13–16).
- When many of Jesus' followers turned away from his difficult teachings, Jesus asked the twelve if they wanted to leave too. Simon Peter answered for the whole group: "Lord, to whom can we go? You have the words of eternal life" (John 6:53–69).
- He was the first to insist that he never would desert Jesus even if everyone else ran away, even if staying with Jesus meant death.
- He was the one who jumped up swinging his sword to defend Jesus in the garden.
- And he, along with John, followed Jesus out of the garden, right into the high priest's courtyard. That took guts.

Yet, when Peter was questioned by a mere servant woman, he panicked. He denied that he even knew Jesus. He repeated the lie, again and again. Then the enormity of his falsehood hit him. He broke down and cried.

Peter's blurting out the wrong thing was nothing new. Jesus had recently reprimanded him for trying to talk Jesus out of putting himself in harm's way by coming here to Jerusalem (Matthew 16:21–23) and for balking when Jesus humbled himself to wash the disciples' feet (John 13:3–9). Peter's mouth was always getting carried away by his zeal for Jesus.

But this time was different. With Jesus in the clutches of his deadly enemies, Peter had shouted *against* him. "No, I'm not a follower of Jesus. No! I don't know the man!"

Peter couldn't kid himself that Jesus would never find out. Jesus had known Peter would deny him before Peter even did it!

So it wasn't merely the danger of being arrested that drove Peter into hiding. It was the reproach he expected to see in the Master's eyes, the sorrowful expression that would say, "How *could* you?"

The Bible doesn't state how long Peter wept, or where. How close to Golgotha was Peter's hideaway? Did the screams, shouts, and laughter reach his ears? Could he overhear snatches of chatter as passersby described how Jesus was flogged, and crowned with thorns, and crucified?

Perhaps, overwhelmed by anxiety and lack of sleep, Simon Peter wept himself into a merciful oblivion and didn't wake up until the body of Jesus had been carried to the tomb.

Happily, we know that Peter didn't destroy himself out of guilt or despair, as Judas did. Perhaps all of Peter's previous gaffes served him well now. He had good reason to hope that forgiveness was possible with Jesus, because he had experienced it firsthand so many times before.

But for a while on that Friday, Peter's bitter remorse had the upper hand.

John, meanwhile, stayed with Jesus throughout his ordeal, to the end on Golgotha. John had always been close to Jesus, like a younger brother. He must have been deeply distressed by the hostile questioning, the scourging and mocking, and the crucifixion.

Yet John apparently made no attempt to intervene. Did he decide it was too dangerous, and ultimately futile, to go up against the Jewish and Roman authorities? Did he sit tight because he expected a fleet of angels to swoop down and pluck Jesus off the cross?

More likely, John knew that Jesus didn't want to be rescued. John had heard Jesus rebuke Peter for trying to protect him from his enemies. And John heard Jesus telling Pilate that his followers would not fight to defend him from the Jewish authorities because his kingdom was not an earthly one.

John did not, however, understand that Jesus' lack of resistance was part of a sacrificial kingdom plan. He didn't figure that out until after the resurrection (John 20:8–9). While he stood by the cross on that awful Friday, John still believed Jesus had intended to establish a political kingdom in Judea—the righteous kingdom spoken of by the prophets (Jeremiah 23:5–6; Isaiah 9:1–7). Now it seemed their kingdom hopes were dying on a cross along with Jesus.

Did John's thoughts turn to the question of succession? With Jesus gone and Peter having turned tail, someone would have to take charge of the ministry. Did John hope that someone would be himself?

Would there even be a ministry left to run, after this disastrous day?

Maybe John pictured himself going back to cleaning nets on his father's fishing boat—quite a comedown, after three glorious years of healing and baptizing and preaching. Was that how it all would end?

Did John begin to wonder if he'd been mistaken in his belief that Jesus was the Messiah? The voice of God in a cloud on the mountaintop had declared that Jesus was his son (Matthew 17:1–5). That was clear proof, wasn't it?

But the truth might not have seemed clear at all to John, at three o'clock that Friday afternoon.

Discussion

1. Followers of Jesus still come under attack from his enemies. What examples have you seen in the news or your own experience?
2. What can we learn from Jesus' disciples about how best to act in the face of persecution?
3. Have you, like Judas Iscariot and Simon Peter, done or said something that caused serious harm to someone else? To someone you loved?

4. Did that person forgive you? Have you forgiven yourself? Do you know, as Peter knew, that there is hope for forgiveness in Jesus?
5. Have you, like John, ever put your faith in a dream that you were sure was God's plan, only to have your expectations crushed? Did you begin to question your faith? Or God's faithfulness?

Closing Prayer

Dear Jesus, thank you for being a loving friend and a patient teacher to us, as you were to your disciples. Remind us to gather together, not scatter apart, when fear and confusion strike. Above all, teach us not to hide from you when we've done wrong, no matter how unpardonable our sin may seem. We look with hope to see forgiveness, not condemnation, in your holy face. Amen.

Song

"God Be with You till We Meet Again" (p. 64/107; all sing)

3

THE WOMEN

Opening Prayer

Savior Jesus, you honored women by making them your apostles in deed, from performing your first public miracle at your mother's request (John 2:1–11) to commissioning Mary Magdalene as the first evangelist to announce your resurrection (John 20:10–18). Teach us now through the Calvary stories of the women who were there. Amen.

Song

"Were You There" (p. 62; all sing)

- When they crucified my Lord?
- When the women wept and wailed?
- When they laid him in the tomb?

Scripture Reading

The following passages are drawn from the gospels of Matthew, Luke, and John. Pay special attention to what they tell us about the women who were there when they crucified our Lord.

After mocking him, they stripped him of the robe and put his own clothes on him. Then they led him away to crucify him. (Matthew 27:31 NRSV)

A great number of the people followed him, and among them were women who were beating their breasts and wailing for him. But Jesus turned to them and said, "Daughters of Jerusalem, do not weep for me, but weep for yourselves and for your children. For the days are surely coming when they will say, 'Blessed are the barren, and the wombs that never bore, and the breasts that never nursed.'" (Luke 23:27–29 NRSV)

When the soldiers had crucified Jesus, they took his clothes and divided them into four parts, one for each soldier. They also took his tunic; now the tunic was seamless, woven in one piece from the top. So they said to one another, "Let us not tear it, but cast lots for it to see who will get it."

And that is what the soldiers did. Meanwhile, standing near the cross of Jesus were his mother, and his mother's sister, Mary the wife of Clopas, and Mary Magdalene. When Jesus saw his mother and the disciple whom he loved standing beside her, he said to his mother, "Woman, here is your son." Then he said to the disciple, "Here is your mother."

> And from that hour the disciple took her into his own home. (John 19:23–27 NRSV)

> Many women were also there, looking on from a distance; they had followed Jesus from Galilee and had provided for him. Among them were Mary Magdalene, and Mary the mother of James and Joseph, and the mother of the sons of Zebedee. When it was evening, there came a rich man from Arimathea, named Joseph, who was also a disciple of Jesus. He went to Pilate and asked for the body of Jesus; then Pilate ordered it to be given to him. So Joseph took the body and wrapped it in a clean linen cloth and laid it in his own new tomb, which he had hewn in the rock. He then rolled a great stone to the door of the tomb and went away. Mary Magdalene and the other Mary were there, sitting opposite the tomb. (Matthew 27:55–61 NRSV)

Meditation

Women of the town wept for Jesus as he dragged his cross through the streets of Jerusalem to the execution place on Golgotha. They formed an escort of official mourners, wailing loudly and beating their breasts with their hands, according to their customs.

We don't know how many of those women knew Jesus personally. Were they sincere in their grief? Or were they merely putting on a show?

What was Jesus' tone of voice when he told them, "Cry for yourselves, not for me"? Pitying? Sardonic?

There also were women on the scene who did know Jesus well. Some had followed him and supported his ministry for many months.

The apostle John's mother was there. She isn't named in the passages we just read, but Mark's gospel (15:40) calls her Salome. This was the wife of Zebedee, not the Salome who danced for Herod and asked for the head of John the Baptist on a platter (Mark 6:17–29). Salome came to Golgotha to support her son John, no doubt, but also because she too was a follower and supporter of Jesus. We know she believed in the coming kingdom of Jesus, because a few days earlier she had accompanied John and his brother, James, to ask Jesus for seats of honor next to his throne (Matthew 20:20–23).

John's gospel mentions the sister of Jesus' mother—Jesus' aunt, in other words. It's commonly thought he was referring to Salome, his own mother, making John and Jesus first cousins. Others believe this sister of Jesus' mother was Mary of Clopas (Cleopas in other translations), who also was reportedly on the scene.

Most of the women watched the crucifixion from a distance. Why didn't they draw near to comfort Jesus?

- Was it too distressing for them to see their beloved teacher's suffering up close?

- Was the scene on Calvary too crowded for the women to push their way closer to the cross?
- Were they kept back by the Roman soldiers?
- Were they intimidated by the presence of openly hostile religious officials?
- Did they fear the rowdy crowd? It's easy to imagine that some of the spectators weren't above mocking and mauling women, especially women who associated with a criminal.

Perhaps most of the women kept their distance out of respect for Jesus' dignity. The Bible repeatedly refers to the shame of Jesus' death on the cross. The whole experience of crucifixion was designed to be degrading, as well as painful and ultimately lethal. This method of execution announced to the world that he had been judged the most despicable sort of criminal. Taking away his clothing, leaving Jesus covered only in his own blood, added to the disgrace.

Roman crosses may not have been as tall as is often depicted in Calvary scenes. Jesus was likely crucified only a foot or two off the ground. Low enough for dogs to sniff and lick at his flesh. Low enough for everyone near the cross to take in every detail of sight, sound, and smell.

There were two women, however, who would not be deterred from approaching the cross. The women closest to Jesus, in death as in life, were Mary his mother and Mary Magdalene, his beloved disciple. These two, along with the apostle John, are often pictured at the foot of the cross.

No one else, not even Jesus' dearest friends, could possibly have felt the grief that his mother felt as she witnessed the agony and death of this miracle child she had birthed and raised. Can we begin to imagine what went through Mary's mind that day?

Remember the seamless tunic the soldiers cast lots for, to avoid cutting it up? Matthew's gospel tells us Jesus was wearing his own clothing when he was sent up the hill to Golgotha from the place where he was scourged. In all likelihood, Jesus' mother had woven that special tunic for him, perhaps as a gift when he went out into the world to begin his ministry. It was a beautiful piece of fine handiwork, woven all in one piece from the top down. That was the distinctive traditional design of tunics woven for a chief priest, not an ordinary carpenter. An interesting statement on the part of the weaver!

Now, on Golgotha, Mary saw that very tunic stained red with her son's blood from the vicious scourging he had endured. She watched the tunic being stripped off Jesus' body by Roman soldiers, who rolled dice to see which of them would keep it for himself. How would it feel to know that the man who had pounded spikes into your son's flesh would strut around the city wearing the tunic you had woven for your son with love in every thread?

The Bible records only a handful of sentences Jesus spoke as he hung on the cross. Every word must have been suffocatingly painful. But when Jesus saw Mary standing near the cross, he summoned the will to speak to John, giving his mother into John's care.

This was not merely a touching sentimental gesture. In ancient Judea, it was vital for a widow to be protected and supported by a son. Jesus made sure that John would fill that role for Mary.

On that Friday, though, Mary might have been supporting John more than the other way around. While the young disciple fretted about what Jesus' arrest and death would mean for his kingdom hopes, Mary was sustained by unwavering confidence that God would fulfill his promise for Jesus to be the savior of the world (Luke 1:26–38; Matthew 1:18–25). She had seen God do the impossible when Jesus was born. God could do the impossible when Jesus died.

Mary Magdalene wept along with Mary and John at the cross. But her tears expressed a very different sense of loss.

Magdalene was one of the women of independent financial means who provided material support for the ministry of Jesus. More importantly, she grew to love him deeply.

Jesus had healed her in body and spirit by casting out seven demons (Luke 8:1–3). He had given back her life. Her identity. An assurance of being utterly loved, after years of being despised and emotionally isolated by her affliction. Now, sympathetic pain for her beloved teacher's suffering must have mixed with a deep, personal fear of abandonment.

While Mary the mother of Jesus was comforted in her grief by her faith in God's power and plan, Mary Magdalene's grief was intensified by turmoil. Mary had peace. Magdalene had questions.

Song

"O My God, Please Tell Me Why" (p. 84/104; female duet)

Meditation (cont.)

Both Marys were devoted to Jesus. Both wept in sorrow and compassion for his suffering. Both knew Jesus did not deserve to be tortured and taunted and executed. Both were powerless to stop it.

Discussion

1. The Bible doesn't tell us whether either of the Marys spoke to Jesus while he hung on the cross. If you were there, what would you say to the dying Jesus?
2. Do you believe, as Jesus' mother did, that God has the power to make the impossible happen for you?
3. Do you express your fears and questions to God honestly, as Mary Magdalene did in the song?

Closing Prayer

Dear Jesus, draw us close to the cross, so that we may better appreciate what you endured for love of us. Give us peace in the sure knowledge that you will never leave us abandoned and unloved. Help us to trust in God's good plan, no matter how desperate the situation seems, for he has the power to make it happen. Amen.

Song

"God Be with You till We Meet Again" (p. 64/107; all sing)

4

THE JEERING CROWD

Opening Prayer

Lord Jesus, during the long hours while you hung nailed to the cross, you were surrounded by on-lookers who watched you suffer and die. Teach us lessons from their stories, as revealed in your Word. Amen.

Song

"Were You There" (p. 62; all sing)

- When they crucified my Lord?
- When they mocked the Son of God?
- When the thief called Jesus "King"?

Scripture Reading

> It was nine o'clock in the morning when they crucified him. The inscription of the charge against him read, "The King of the Jews." And with him they crucified two bandits, one on his right and one on his left. Those who passed by derided him, shaking their heads

> and saying, "Aha! You who would destroy the temple and build it in three days, save yourself, and come down from the cross!" In the same way the chief priests, along with the scribes, were also mocking him among themselves and saying, "He saved others; he cannot save himself. Let the Messiah, the King of Israel, come down from the cross now, so that we may see and believe." Those who were crucified with him also taunted him. (Mark 15:25–32 NRSV)

> One of the criminals who were hanged there kept deriding him and saying, "Are you not the Messiah? Save yourself and us!" But the other rebuked him, saying, "Do you not fear God, since you are under the same sentence of condemnation? And we indeed have been condemned justly, for we are getting what we deserve for our deeds, but this man has done nothing wrong." Then he said, "Jesus, remember me when you come into your kingdom." He replied, "Truly I tell you, today you will be with me in Paradise." (Luke 23:39–43 NRSV)

Meditation

In our study of the scene at Golgotha, we've looked at Roman soldiers, the apostle John, Mary Magdalene, Mary the mother of Jesus, and several other women who were followers of Jesus.

Crowds of other onlookers were there that day, too. The location of Golgotha was close to Jerusalem, and the city was overflowing with Jews who had traveled to celebrate the Passover. There was no shortage of interested people.

Imagine the great hubbub around Golgotha, the jostling and shouting, the buzz of gossip making the rounds. Everyone was eager to get—or give—the gory details. Some described how Jesus was apprehended and questioned and scourged. Some talked about his long trudge up the hill, carrying his own cross. Some whispered about the special tunic the soldiers had confiscated. Some spoke, with either horror or relish, of the spikes being pounded through flesh into wood.

No doubt, these reports strayed further from the facts with every retelling. Distorted stories about Jesus' activities during his three years of public ministry probably spread like a virus, too. Spectators and passersby shouted insults at Jesus, twisting his words and throwing them back in his face.

The loudest voices taunting Jesus belonged to the religious leaders, the chief priests and teachers of the Jewish Law. Threatened by Jesus' popularity, they had falsely accused him of stirring up a revolt against the Roman Emperor, Caesar. Their strategy to have Jesus crucified by the Romans had worked to perfection. Now they came to Golgotha to gloat.

Center stage along with Jesus were two thieves who also had been crucified that day. These men had not been picked up for shoplifting sandals from the local marketplace. No, they were notorious bandits, convicted of armed robbery. Yet they had the gall to mock Jesus too.

One robber jeered, "Save me, if you're the Messiah." Little did he realize, that's exactly what Jesus was in the process of doing!

The other robber also taunted Jesus. But suddenly he had a change of heart. We can only wonder what prompted it.

- Did the crowd's chatter about Jesus' healing and teaching and raising the dead convince him that Jesus really was the Messiah?
- Did he overhear a couple of chief priests congratulating each other for successfully railroading Jesus?
- Did it cross his mind that cracking Son of God jokes might not be a smart move for someone who's about to meet God face to face?

Whatever the reason, this thief finally had enough of the other fellow's loud contempt for God and decided to speak up for Jesus. He admitted that he himself was guilty and declared that Jesus was innocent. Not only innocent, but coming into a kingdom!

What a bizarre thing to believe about a man who obviously will soon die a shameful death on a cross! But because the repentant thief did believe, he called on Jesus for favor.

Song

"Jesus, Please Remember Me" (p. 88/90/101; male solo or all sing)

Meditation (cont.)

The crucified robber who believed in Jesus pleaded, "Remember me." What response did he receive from Jesus?

Reunion in Paradise.

Less than twenty-four hours earlier, at his last supper with the twelve, Jesus had pleaded for remembrance (Luke 22:14–20). What response had *he* received?

- Betrayal by Judas Iscariot
- Denial by Simon Peter
- Desertion by all but one of the rest

Still, there must have been others in the crowd of spectators on Calvary, besides the repentant thief, who felt sympathy for Jesus. Surely *some* people there knew that Jesus had been preaching the word of God and doing good, not plotting a political revolution.

What about Nicodemus, the member of the Jewish ruling council who had tried unsuccessfully to derail the council's conspiracy to execute Jesus? We know that Nicodemus came to Calvary later that Friday, after Jesus was dead. He helped take Jesus down from the cross and carry him to the tomb. He brought myrrh and aloes to anoint the body for burial (John 19:38–42). Had Nicodemus been there the whole day? Was he standing among his council colleagues while they mocked the crucified Jesus?

Or did he lie low until the bloodthirsty mob had gone home, as he had waited until nightfall to visit Jesus as a disciple? In secret, Nicodemus had said, "Rabbi, we know that you are a teacher who has come from God. For no one could perform the signs you are doing if God were not with him" (John 3:1–2 NIV). Did he also come in secret to prepare Jesus for burial?

Where were all the lepers and blind and crippled and sick Jesus had healed—even raised from the dead? Where were the five thousand he'd fed from one boy's lunch of bread and fish (John 6:1–14)? What about the thousands who had witnessed other miracles Jesus had performed in his three years of public ministry? And the excited throng who'd shouted "Hosanna!" when he rode into Jerusalem on a donkey a few days earlier (Matthew 21:1–11)?

Many of those witnesses and adoring fans must have been in Jerusalem that Friday, being either residents or visitors for the Passover celebration. Some of them must have heard that Jesus had been arrested and sentenced to die. Some must have made their way to Calvary to see the situation for themselves.

How many of them were there, listening to the godly teacher Jesus of Nazareth being mocked and watching him being tortured and crucified unjustly?

How many of them were there and kept silent? How many of them were there and hurled insults at Jesus, along with the rest of the mob?

Discussion

1. Has anyone ever taunted or bullied you when you were down and out, as the jeering onlookers did to Jesus? How does being treated that way make you feel?
2. Think about the spectators at Calvary who had previously cheered for Jesus and witnessed his miracles. What reasons might they give for keeping silent? For joining in the mockery?
3. Have you ever felt you had to hide your true beliefs from leaders and others in your faith community, as Nicodemus did? Why?

Closing Prayer

Jesus, we confess that we don't always speak up for you when you are mocked and your offer of salvation is belittled. Too often, we ourselves fail to give you the honor you are due. Forgive us, Son of God. Have mercy, and remember us with favor. Amen.

Song

"God Be with You till We Meet Again" (p. 64/107; all sing)

5

THE UNSEEN PRESENCE

Opening Prayer

Precious Savior Jesus, we can't fully fathom what you did for us on the cross. Open our minds and touch our hearts with a little more understanding, that we may be moved to greater joy in your gift and greater gratitude to you. Amen.

Song

"Were You There" (p. 62; all sing)

- When they crucified my Lord?
- When he cried, "My God, my God"?
- When the earth began to quake?

Meditation

We've seen a whole cast of characters on Calvary:

- The Roman soldiers who carried out Pontius Pilate's order of execution
- The apostle John
- Mary the mother of Jesus and the other women

- Two thieves crucified alongside Jesus
- The religious leaders who had plotted Jesus' destruction and showed up to heckle him
- The jostling, jeering crowd

Have we missed anyone? Who else was there when the Son of God was crucified?

What about the Lord God, whose plan brought Jesus Christ and all the others to Calvary in the first place?

Scripture Reading

> Now the birth of Jesus the Messiah took place in this way. When his mother Mary had been engaged to Joseph, but before they lived together, she was found to be with child from the Holy Spirit. Her husband Joseph, being a righteous man and unwilling to expose her to public disgrace, planned to dismiss her quietly. But just when he had resolved to do this, an angel of the Lord appeared to him in a dream and said, "Joseph, son of David, do not be afraid to take Mary as your wife, for the child conceived in her is from the Holy Spirit. She will bear a son, and you are to name him Jesus, for he will save his people from their sins." (Matthew 1:18–21 NRSV)

> "For God so loved the world that he gave his only Son, so that everyone who believes in him may not perish but may have eternal life.

> Indeed, God did not send the Son into the world to condemn the world, but in order that the world might be saved through him." (John 3:16–17 NRSV)
>
> When we were utterly helpless, Christ came at just the right time and died for us sinners. Now, most people would not be willing to die for an upright person, though someone might perhaps be willing to die for a person who is especially good. But God showed his great love for us by sending Christ to die for us while we were still sinners. (Romans 5:6–8 NLT)

Meditation (cont.)

According to these and other scriptures, it was by God's plan that Jesus came into the world, born as a human being. And it was by God's plan that Jesus suffered and died as a human being, to bring about reconciliation between the sinful human race and our supremely holy creator.

Wouldn't God want to be there to witness the climax of his grand design?

Scripture Reading

> When it was noon, darkness came over the whole land until three in the afternoon. At three o'clock Jesus cried out with a loud voice, "Eloi, Eloi, lema sabachthani?" which means, "My God, my God, why have you forsaken

me?" When some of the bystanders heard it, they said, "Listen, he is calling for Elijah." And someone ran, filled a sponge with sour wine, put it on a stick, and gave it to him to drink, saying, "Wait, let us see whether Elijah will come to take him down." Then Jesus gave a loud cry and breathed his last. And the curtain of the temple was torn in two, from top to bottom. Now when the centurion, who stood facing him, saw that in this way he breathed his last, he said, "Truly this man was God's Son!" (Mark 15:33–39 NRSV)

Meditation (cont.)

God's purpose in bringing Jesus to Calvary is clearly shown in the scriptures. God's presence there is not so clear.

A powerful divine presence was suggested by the strange phenomena that occurred that day:

- Darkness overshadowed the scene.
- An earthquake rocked Golgotha, splitting the earth and opening tombs.
- The temple veil was torn from top to bottom.

But God the Father was not seen. God the Father's voice was not heard.

Remember the voice that spoke from a mysterious cloud when Jesus was baptized (Matthew 3:17) and again when he was transfigured on the mountaintop (Matthew 17:5)?

The voice had proclaimed, "This is my beloved Son, in whom I am well pleased" (NRSV).

Wouldn't that Friday morning have been a great time for an encore? But God did not refute the accusations of Jesus' enemies with a booming endorsement in front of the crowd on Golgotha.

In fact, the plaintive cry of the crucified Jesus suggests that God the Father wasn't there at all.

"My God, my God, why have you forsaken me?"

It can't be coincidence that these are the opening words of Psalm 22. Even though David wrote them many years before the birth of Jesus Christ, verses in Psalm 22 could have been pulled straight out of the crucifixion scene on Calvary.

Scripture Reading

> All who see me mock me; they hurl insults, shaking their heads. "He trusts in the Lord," they say, "let the Lord rescue him. Let him deliver him, since he delights in him." (Psalm 22:7–8 NIV)

> Dogs surround me, a pack of villains encircles me; they pierce my hands and my feet. All my bones are on display; people stare and gloat over me. They divide my clothes among them and cast lots for my garment. (Psalm 22:16–18 NIV)

Meditation (cont.)

Jesus knew the scriptures well. He surely was familiar with this psalm written by his famous ancestor. Did he cry out "My God, my God, why have you forsaken me?" because David's desperate prayer resonated so closely with his own circumstances? In other words, was Jesus using the language of abandonment figuratively, to express the depth of his agony as he neared death?

Or was Jesus literally forsaken by God at that moment? Should we count God the Father among those who were conspicuous by their absence from Calvary when they crucified our Lord?

God the Father loved Jesus dearly. The two were in constant communication. Why, then, would God turn his back on Jesus now, at the height of his suffering? Surely this was the very time Jesus needed God's presence most!

Perhaps this also was the very time Jesus needed God's *absence* most.

By leaving Jesus on his own to die a fully human, fully voluntary death, the Father assured that Jesus would receive full honor and glory for his sacrifice. No one could diminish Jesus' ordeal by pointing to a divine hand shielding him from the whip. No army of angels shared the weight of the cross he carried to Golgotha. No miraculous nerve-block numbed the pain of spikes driven through his flesh and bones. Jesus took the full brunt himself.

But Jesus' sacrifice went far beyond the obvious suffering of torture and death. On top of excruciating physical pain, he suffered the spiritual pain of condemnation for the sins of the whole world. All of them—past, present, and future. What a ghastly burden! Did God turn his face away because the load of guilt Jesus carried was too monstrous, too unholy for the supremely holy God to look upon?

Separation from God has been called the very essence of hell and damnation. If that is so, perhaps his condemnation for the sins of humankind separated Jesus from God. Forsaken, indeed!

Jesus had freely accepted the condemnation. But, even if he knew beforehand that the estrangement from his Father was going to happen, that wouldn't make it any easier to bear. The desolation of being forsaken by God in his moment of trial had to be the worst suffering of all.

Song

"My God, Why" (p. 92/102; expressive solo)

or "Where Are You, My God" (p. 94/116; all sing)

Meditation (cont.)

Good news! If God did indeed hide his face from Jesus while he hung on the cross, he wasn't far away. He saw everything his beloved son suffered in obedience to his will. He heard him cry out in agony.

God heard Jesus cry out in victory, too. The mission was accomplished, and the Father was well pleased.

Discussion

1. Has God given you a mission? Have you sensed the presence of God watching over you as you carried out his work? Does he seem close or sometimes far away?
2. Have you ever felt as if God abandoned you when your mission ran into difficulties?
3. Has a Bible verse or hymn ever strengthened you by expressing what you're going through?
4. Our closing song is "God Be with You till We Meet Again." What do you think is the significance of asking God to "be with" a person?

Closing Prayer

O God, you are the unseen presence who watches over all your children. If it pleases you, allow us to experience your supportive presence, especially when we go through times of suffering. Thank you for loving us so much that you reconciled us to yourself through your beloved son, Jesus, in whose name we pray. Amen.

Song

"God Be with You till We Meet Again" (p. 64/107; all sing)

6

THE REDEEMED

Opening Prayer

Savior Jesus, you teach us by example to love generously and obey God faithfully. In spite of our failings—indeed, because of our failings—we beg you to count us among the friends for whom you laid down your life in love. Amen.

Meditation

We're making our last visit to the scene of Jesus' crucifixion. We've looked at the Roman authorities, the religious leaders, the soldiers, the apostles, the women, the crucified thieves, and all the spectators who were present on Calvary—even God himself.

There is one more presence to consider.

Look around. Not around Golgotha, but around this room. Were *you* there when they crucified our Lord?

None of us could have been there physically, of course. Those events happened two thousand years ago, in a land many miles away. And yet . . .

In a sense, people of every time and place were there.

- In our oblivion to spiritual dangers, weren't we all there sleeping in the garden when Jesus told his disciples to stay alert and pray, so they would not fall into temptation?
- In our fear, weren't we all there when Jesus' disciples ran away and Simon Peter denied knowing him?
- In our willingness to sacrifice other people to further our selfish agendas, weren't we all there when Judas betrayed Jesus and Pontius Pilate handed him over to be crucified, knowing him to be innocent?
- In our collective guilt for the sins Jesus died to pardon, weren't we all there with the Roman soldiers, lashing Jesus with a whip? Pounding nails into his hands and feet? Piercing his heart?
- In our grieving and in our mutual love and support, weren't we all there at the foot of the cross with John and the two Marys?
- In our hope for mercy and favor, weren't we all there with the crucified thief, pleading, "Jesus, remember me"?
- In God's will for our redemption through Jesus' suffering and death and in the free choice to accept or reject that great gift, weren't we all there in the crowd at Calvary?

Song

"We Were All There" (p. 98/108; all sing)

Meditation (cont.)

Ah, finally we shift our eyes from the cross to the empty tomb! We can stop trembling with fear and tremble instead with awe at God's mighty work in raising Jesus in victory. Our Savior lives! The kingdom is at hand!

In God's will for our redemption, we are there, not only for Jesus' suffering and death but also for his resurrection. The Bible confirms that hope.

Scripture Reading

> Do you not know that all of us who have been baptized into Christ Jesus were baptized into his death? Therefore we have been buried with him by baptism into death, so that, just as Christ was raised from the dead by the glory of the Father, so we too might walk in newness of life. For if we have been united with him in a death like his, we will certainly be united with him in a resurrection like his. (Romans 6:3–5 NRSV)

Our final scripture readings, drawn from the gospels of Matthew and John, describe Jesus' resurrection and the immediate aftermath.

> After the Sabbath, at dawn on the first day of the week, Mary Magdalene and the other Mary

went to look at the tomb. There was a violent earthquake, for an angel of the Lord came down from heaven and, going to the tomb, rolled back the stone and sat on it. His appearance was like lightning, and his clothes were white as snow. The guards were so afraid of him that they shook and became like dead men.

The angel said to the women, "Do not be afraid, for I know that you are looking for Jesus, who was crucified. He is not here; he has risen, just as he said. Come and see the place where he lay. Then go quickly and tell his disciples: 'He has risen from the dead and is going ahead of you into Galilee. There you will see him.' Now I have told you." So the women hurried away from the tomb, afraid yet filled with joy, and ran to tell his disciples.

While the women were on their way, some of the guards went into the city and reported to the chief priests everything that had happened. When the chief priests had met with the elders and devised a plan, they gave the soldiers a large sum of money, telling them, "You are to say, 'His disciples came during the night and stole him away while we were asleep.' If this report gets to the governor, we will satisfy him and keep you out of trouble." So the soldiers took the money and did as they were instructed. And this story has been widely circulated among the Jews to this very day. (Matthew 28:1–8, 11–15 NIV)

Early on the first day of the week, while it was still dark, Mary Magdalene went to the tomb and saw that the stone had been removed from the entrance. So she came running to Simon Peter and the other disciple, the one Jesus loved, and said, "They have taken the Lord out of the tomb, and we don't know where they have put him!"

So Peter and the other disciple started for the tomb. Both were running, but the other disciple outran Peter and reached the tomb first. He bent over and looked in at the strips of linen lying there but did not go in. Then Simon Peter came along behind him and went straight into the tomb. He saw the strips of linen lying there, as well as the cloth that had been wrapped around Jesus' head. The cloth was still lying in its place, separate from the linen. Finally the other disciple, who had reached the tomb first, also went inside. He saw and believed. (They still did not understand from Scripture that Jesus had to rise from the dead.) Then the disciples went back to where they were staying.

Now Mary stood outside the tomb crying. As she wept, she bent over to look into the tomb and saw two angels in white, seated where Jesus' body had been, one at the head and the other at the foot.

They asked her, "Woman, why are you crying?"

"They have taken my Lord away," she said, "and I don't know where they have put him." At this, she turned around and saw Jesus standing there, but she did not realize that it was Jesus.

He asked her, "Woman, why are you crying? Who is it you are looking for?"

Thinking he was the gardener, she said, "Sir, if you have carried him away, tell me where you have put him, and I will get him."

Jesus said to her, "Mary."

She turned toward him and cried out in Aramaic, "Rabboni!" (which means "Teacher").

Jesus said, "Do not hold on to me, for I have not yet ascended to the Father. Go instead to my brothers and tell them, 'I am ascending to my Father and your Father, to my God and your God.'"

Mary Magdalene went to the disciples with the news: "I have seen the Lord!" And she told them that he had said these things to her.

On the evening of that first day of the week, when the disciples were together, with the doors locked for fear of the Jewish leaders, Jesus came and stood among them and said,

> "Peace be with you!" After he said this, he showed them his hands and side. The disciples were overjoyed when they saw the Lord. (John 20:1–20 NIV)

Song

"Roll the Stone Away" (p. 96/106; all sing)

Meditation (cont.)

We are blessed to have the perspective of knowing what happened after Jesus suffered and died. We know that John's kingdom hopes didn't die on the cross; they were fulfilled in the empty tomb. We know that Mary Magdalene was not abandoned by Jesus; their relationship was elevated to an eternal bond by his death and resurrection.

All of us can share that bond if we so choose. And because Jesus lives today, we know that someone is listening when we call on Jesus' name, as the repentant thief did.

Yes, Jesus will remember us.

Will *we* remember *him*?

Closing Prayer

Lord Jesus, you suffered through a terrible ordeal before emerging victorious from the grave. Having dwelt for a short time in the shadow of the cross, may we emerge with deeper appreciation for your suffering and more extravagant joy in the victorious life you gained for us. All thanks, praise, and honor forever be yours. Amen.

Song

"God Be with You till We Meet Again" (p. 64/107; all sing)

SONGS

MUSIC NOTES

"Were You There" serves as the opening song for the first five sessions. The three verses for each session are outlined on the page facing the score. Each session closes with the first verse of "God Be with You till We Meet Again."

"Who Is This Man" is a narrative song written for an expressive soloist representing a Roman soldier. To help the singer stay on track, his score is laid out with one full verse per page.

Note that "Who Is This Man" has fewer melismas (syllables sung across multiple notes) than familiar hymns with the same melody. Be ready to deliver a few rapid-fire sequences, especially in the middle of the next-to-last line of each verse (e.g., "stretched his arms so wide" in verse 4). Be alert for pairs of eighth notes that have a melisma in some verses but not in others.

Vary your vocal and instrumental dynamics throughout the song to express the emotion of the story (and to avoid boring listeners with thirteen identical repetitions of the tune!). For example, a guitarist can dramatize the sudden earthquake with percussive dry strumming at the beginning of verse 11. The most important pauses are marked on the score near the end of the tenth verse (the death of Jesus).

A sheet with suggested chords for "Who Is This Man" follows the singer's score. Other chords and piano accompaniments for this tune (LAZARUS) can be found under the more recent tune name KINGSFOLD in many hymnals and online resources.

"Jesus, Please Remember Me" can be sung as a solo or a group song. When presenting it as a solo, tailor the delivery to the lyrics for maximum impact. Two scores are provided. The first includes lyrics, melody, and chords. The second has harmony notes for group singing and/or piano accompaniment.

"Where Were the Twelve" comes in two settings. Choose either a plain hymn tune or a round.

"Oh, My God, Please Tell Me Why" is a female duet. The soprano representing Magdalene sings only the odd-numbered verses, always on the melody line. The singer representing Mary the mother of Jesus sings the even-numbered verses plus the seventh verse.

If possible, sing mother Mary's verses on the alto line (which has been modified to be a bit more tuneful than the standard alto line). In addition to making the tune less repetitious, this contrast helps listeners follow the give-and-take between the two women and also creates a nice harmony when their voices join for the last verse.

"My God, Why" is a dramatic narrative solo for a capable, expressive vocalist. The three opening words of each verse deserve special attention. Give every syllable its due. The slow, haunting melody is excerpted from John Dowland's secular air "Time Stands Still." Dowland's original music called for a lute and a bass viol. Several accompaniments using modern instruments are posted on the Audio page at LindaBonneyOlin.com. Adapt them to your own musical resources and preferences, and look online for other options. Or, for a simpler song, choose the group hymn "Where Are You, My God" instead.

For easy reading, complete lyrics of all the songs in this book are provided in text-only format, beginning on page 101. Poetry fans might enjoy taking a closer look at the lyrics of "My God, Why." Its unusual rhyme scheme is more evident when the text stands alone on the page.

Visit www.LindaBonneyOlin.com for helpful music resources.

Were You There

Traditional, alt. African-American spiritual

1. Were you there when they cru-ci-fied my Lord?
Were you there when they cru-ci-fied my Lord?
Oh! . Some-times it caus-es me to
trem-ble, trem-ble, trem-ble.
Were you there when they cru-ci-fied my Lord?

Chapter 1 When they crucified my Lord?
When the sun refused to shine?
When they pierced him in the side?

Chapter 2 When they crucified my Lord?
When his friends all ran away?
When they nailed him to the tree?

Chapter 3 When they crucified my Lord?
When the women wept and wailed?
When they laid him in the tomb?

Chapter 4 When they crucified my Lord?
When they mocked the Son of God?
When the thief called Jesus "King"?

Chapter 5 When they crucified my Lord?
When he cried, "My God, my God"?
When the earth began to quake?

God Be with You till We Meet Again

Jeremiah E. Rankin, 1880 William Gould Tomer, 1880

God be with you till we meet a - gain;
by his coun-sels guide, up - hold you,
with his sheep se - cure - ly fold you;
God be with you till we meet a - gain.

Till we meet, till we meet, till we
till we meet, till we meet a - gain,

meet at Je - sus' feet; till we
Till we meet

meet, till we meet,
till we meet, till we meet a - gain

God be with you till we meet a - gain.

Who Is This Man

Linda Bonney Olin, 2016   Traditional English tune (LAZARUS)

♩= 96
1. I was there the day that Je - sus died.
I will sim - ply tell what I saw.
All of you, when I have tes - ti - fied,
may your own con - clu - sions draw.
You should know that I did not mere-ly see
what tran - spired on Gol - go - tha hill.
It was my own hand that nailed him to the tree,
and that knowl - edge haunts_ me still.

2. I'm a Ro - man sol - dier. I o - bey
with-out ques - tion eve-ry com - mand.
And the or - der Pi - late gave that day
was to cru - ci - fy___ a man.
Yes, a Jew named Je-sus the Naz - a - rene
was con - demned on the cross to die.
I in - scribed the charg-es to be plain - ly seen:
"King of Jews." I'll tell___ you why.

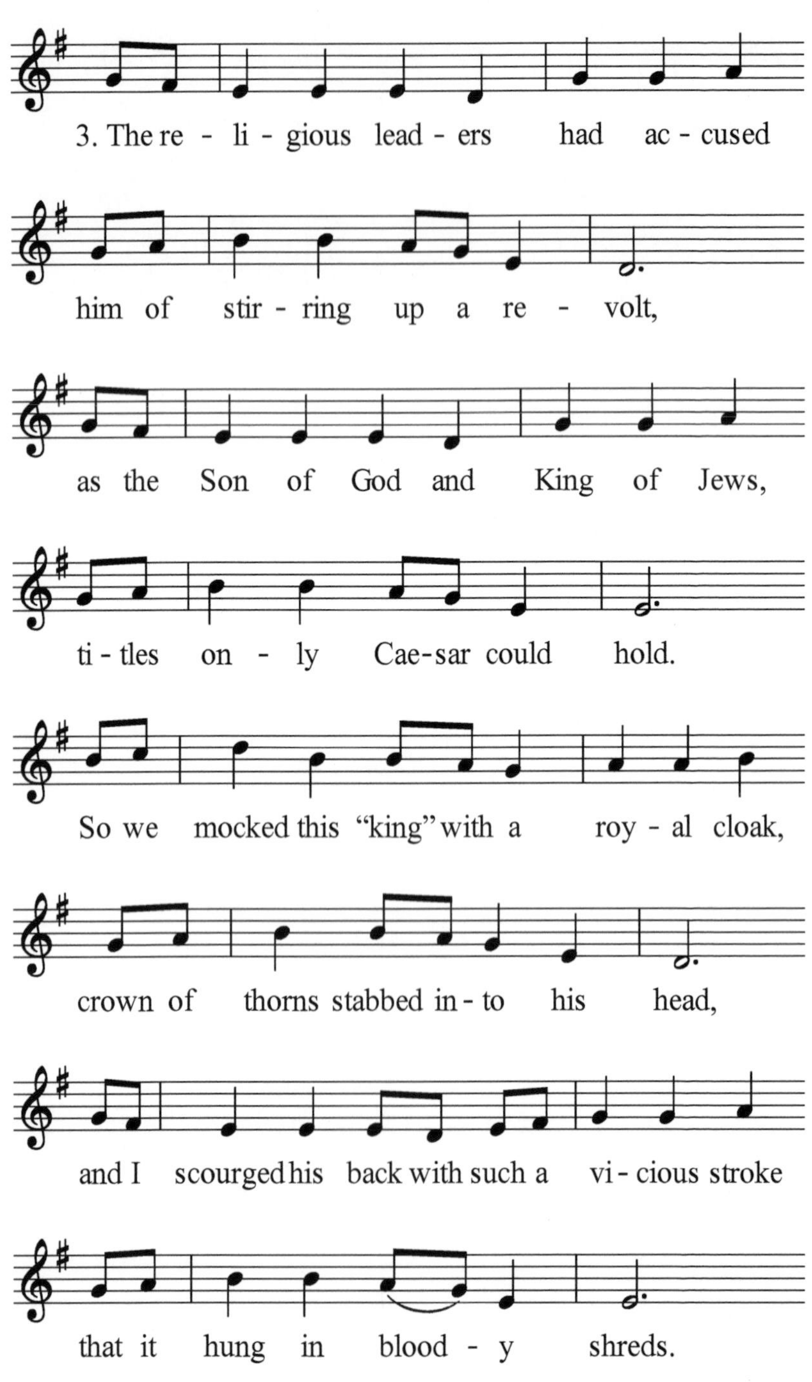
3. The re - li - gious lead - ers had ac - cused
him of stir - ring up a re - volt,
as the Son of God and King of Jews,
ti - tles on - ly Cae-sar could hold.
So we mocked this "king" with a roy - al cloak,
crown of thorns stabbed in - to his head,
and I scourged his back with such a vi - cious stroke
that it hung in blood - y shreds.

4. Did that both - er me? No, not at all.
I had scourged men hun-dreds of times.
That's the price, by Ro - man pro - to - col,
con-victs pay for ter - ri - ble crimes.
We made Je - sus shoul-der a heav - y beam.
To Gol - go - tha he bore its weight.
There he fell and stretched his arms so wide, it seemed
he em - braced his com - ing fate.

5. When I pressed his hands a - gainst the wood
and be - gan to ham-mer the spikes,
far from curs-ing me, as some men would,
he looked deep in - to my eyes.
"Fa-ther, please for-give them for what they do,
for they don't un-der-stand," he cried.
I just pound-ed hard-er, for I thought I knew
he was just - ly cru - ci - fied.

6. When we hoist-ed Je - sus' cross in place,
eve-ry nail ripped through his flesh more.
There he hung in tor - ment and dis - grace,
but such things I'd learned to ig - nore.
Hav-ing stripped our pris-on-ers' cloth-ing off,
we di - vid - ed the goods we'd seized.
But for Je - sus' tu-nic we in - stead cast lots,
for it was one seam - less piece.

7. Nine o' - clock: Three cru - ci - fix - ions done,
Je - sus plus two dan - ger - ous thieves.
We four sol - diers, the cen - tu - ri - on,
and the jeer - ing crowd__ were pleased.
Heck - lers called, "Hail, King of the Jews!" with glee.
"Save your - self, Son of God Most High!"
"Yes, Mes - si - ah! Save your - self, and then save me,"
mocked a thief who hung at his side.

8. But the sec - ond thief re - buked the first.
"Don't you fear God's pun - ish - ment?
We are guilt - y and de - serve the worst,
but this man is in - no - cent."
Then he said to Je - sus, "Re - mem - ber me
in your king - dom," to my sur - prise.
Je-sus an - swered, "Tru - ly I say you will meet
me to - day in par - a - dise!"

9. Je - sus, in - no - cent? He'd had a trial.
Pi - late must have had a good cause.
But there hap-pened, in a lit - tle while,
strange e - vents that gave_ me pause.
Close to noon the sky be-gan turn - ing black,
though I'd not seen a sin - gle cloud.
Light-ning flashed a-bove us, and the thun-der cracked.
Three o' - clock: Je-sus cried_ out loud.

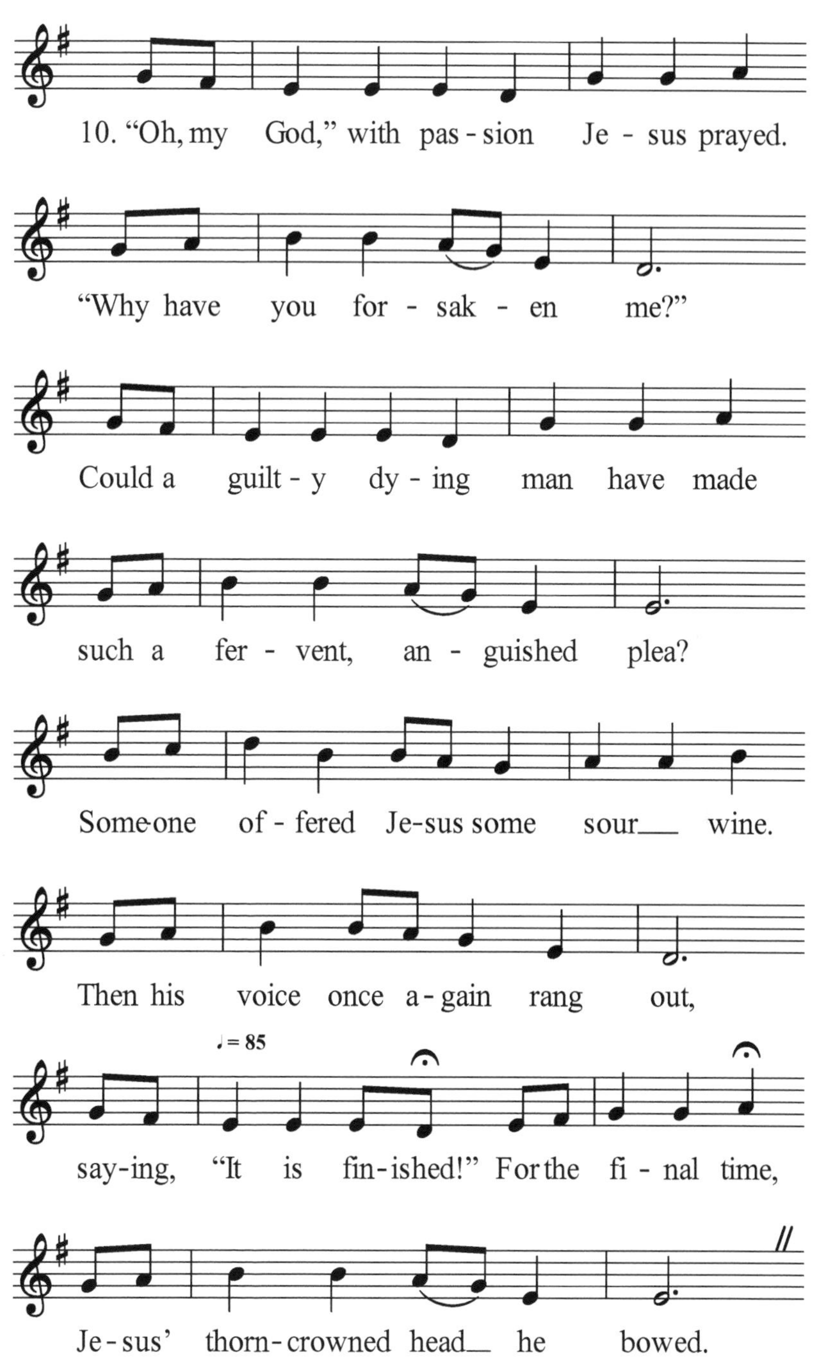
10. "Oh, my God," with pas - sion Je - sus prayed.
"Why have you for - sak - en me?"
Could a guilt - y dy - ing man have made
such a fer - vent, an - guished plea?
Some-one of - fered Je-sus some sour__ wine.
Then his voice once a - gain rang out,
♩ = 85
say-ing, "It is fin-ished!" For the fi - nal time,
Je - sus' thorn-crowned head__ he bowed.

♩ = 96
11. All at once, I felt Gol - go - tha shake.
Boul ders split and crashed on the ground.
Peo-ple try - ing to es - cape the quake
in a pan - ic stum-bled a - round.
Though a sol - dier al-ways must be pre-pared,
by this pow'r we were o - ver - awed.
The cen - tu - ri - on, up-on his knees, de-clared,
"Tru-ly, he was the Son__ of God!"

12. When the rock - ing earth grew calm, I found
both the rob - bers still were a - live.
They must die be - fore the sun went down
and the Jew - ish Sab-bath ar - rived.
So we broke their legs, that the end be rushed;
but for Je - sus I raised my spear.
When I pierced his side, both blood and wa - ter gushed.
He was dead. That was ver - y clear.
13. Two men, bring - ing oint-ments and per - fume,

took the bod - y down from the cross.
Then they placed it in a near - by tomb,
and we rolled a stone_ a - cross.
Soon the sun went down and the day was done,
but I still did-n't un - der - stand.
Were we sol-diers stand-ing watch on God's own son?
Who_ was— Who is___ this man?
Were we sol-diers stand-ing watch on God's own son?
Who_ was — Who *is*___ this man?

WHO IS THIS MAN

CHORD SHEET

Where Were the Twelve

Linda Bonney Olin, 2016 William Gardiner's *Sacred Melodies*
1815 (GERMANY)

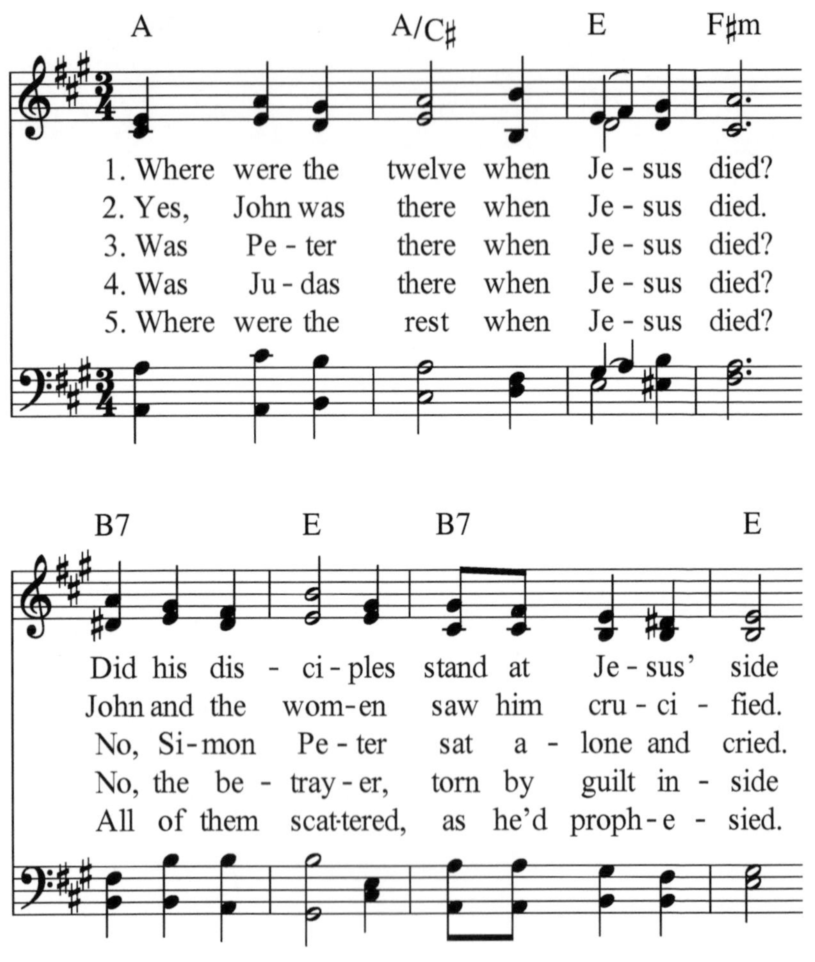
A A/C♯ E F♯m
1. Where were the twelve when Je - sus died?
2. Yes, John was there when Je - sus died.
3. Was Pe - ter there when Je - sus died?
4. Was Ju - das there when Je - sus died?
5. Where were the rest when Je - sus died?
B7 E B7 E
Did his dis - ci - ples stand at Je - sus' side
John and the wom - en saw him cru - ci - fied.
No, Si - mon Pe - ter sat a - lone and cried.
No, the be - tray - er, torn by guilt in - side
All of them scat-tered, as he'd proph - e - sied.

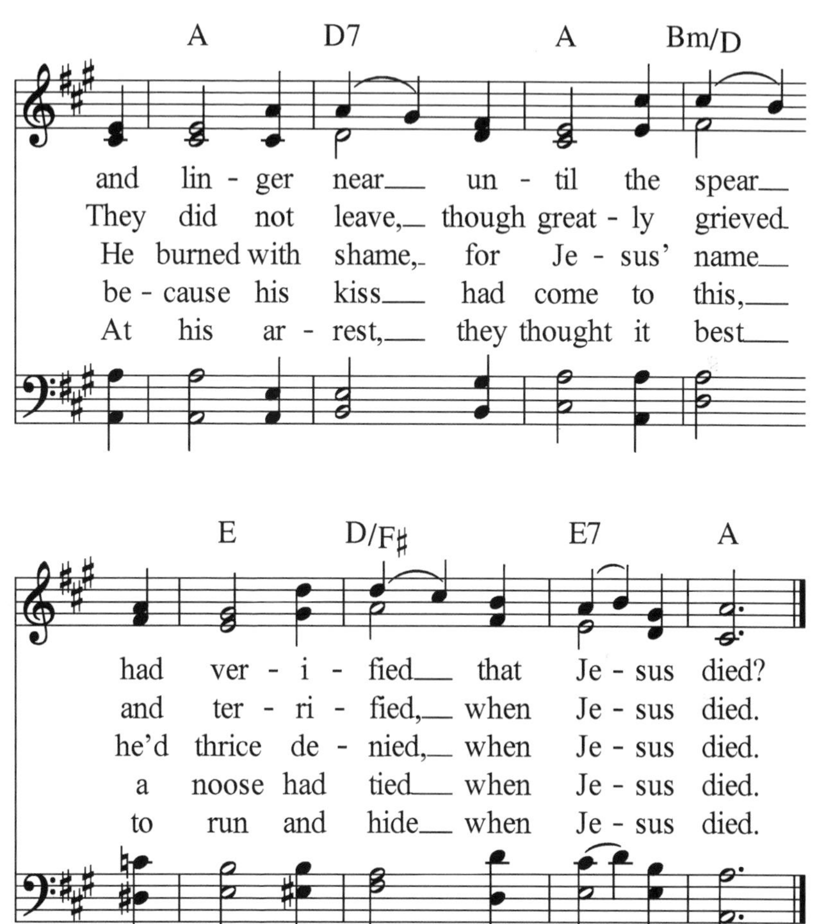
A D7 A Bm/D
and lin - ger near un - til the spear
They did not leave, though great - ly grieved.
He burned with shame, for Je - sus' name
be - cause his kiss had come to this,
At his ar - rest, they thought it best
E D/F♯ E7 A
had ver - i - fied that Je - sus died?
and ter - ri - fied, when Je - sus died.
he'd thrice de - nied, when Je - sus died.
a noose had tied when Je - sus died.
to run and hide when Je - sus died.

Where Were the Twelve (Round)

Linda Bonney Olin, 2016

Thomas Tallis, c. 1561
(TALLIS' CANON)

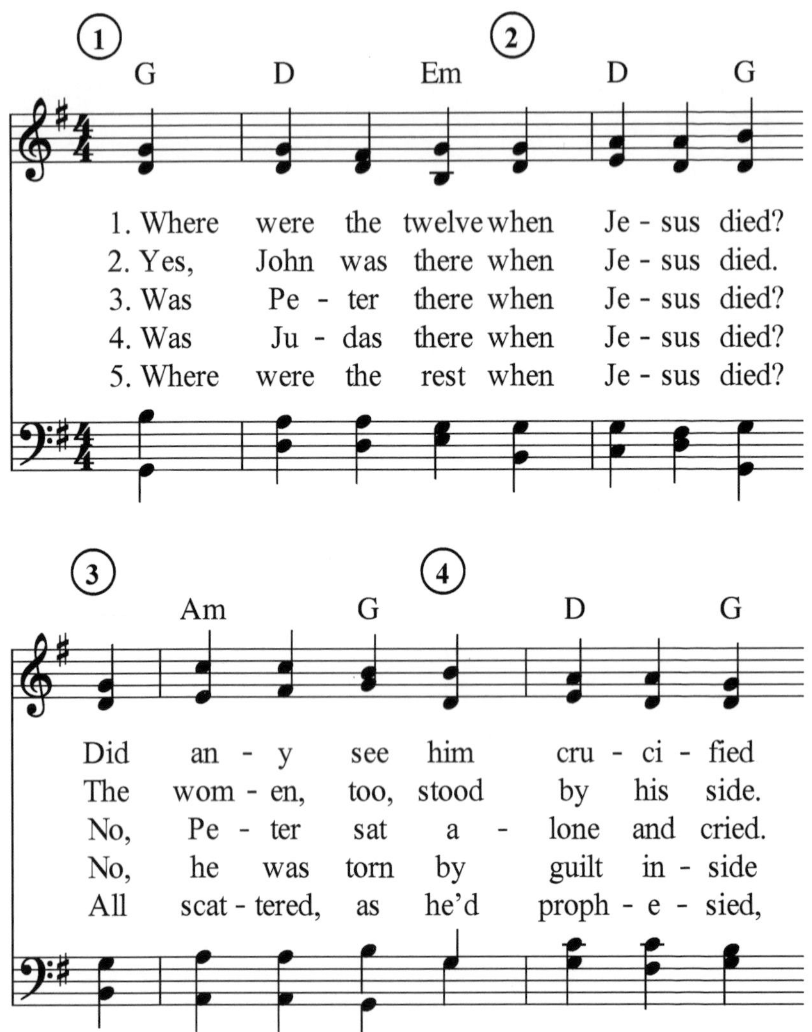

1
2
G D Em D G
1. Where were the twelve when Je - sus died?
2. Yes, John was there when Je - sus died.
3. Was Pe - ter there when Je - sus died?
4. Was Ju - das there when Je - sus died?
5. Where were the rest when Je - sus died?
3
4
Am G D G
Did an - y see him cru - ci - fied
The wom - en, too, stood by his side.
No, Pe - ter sat a - lone and cried.
No, he was torn by guilt in - side
All scat - tered, as he'd proph - e - sied,

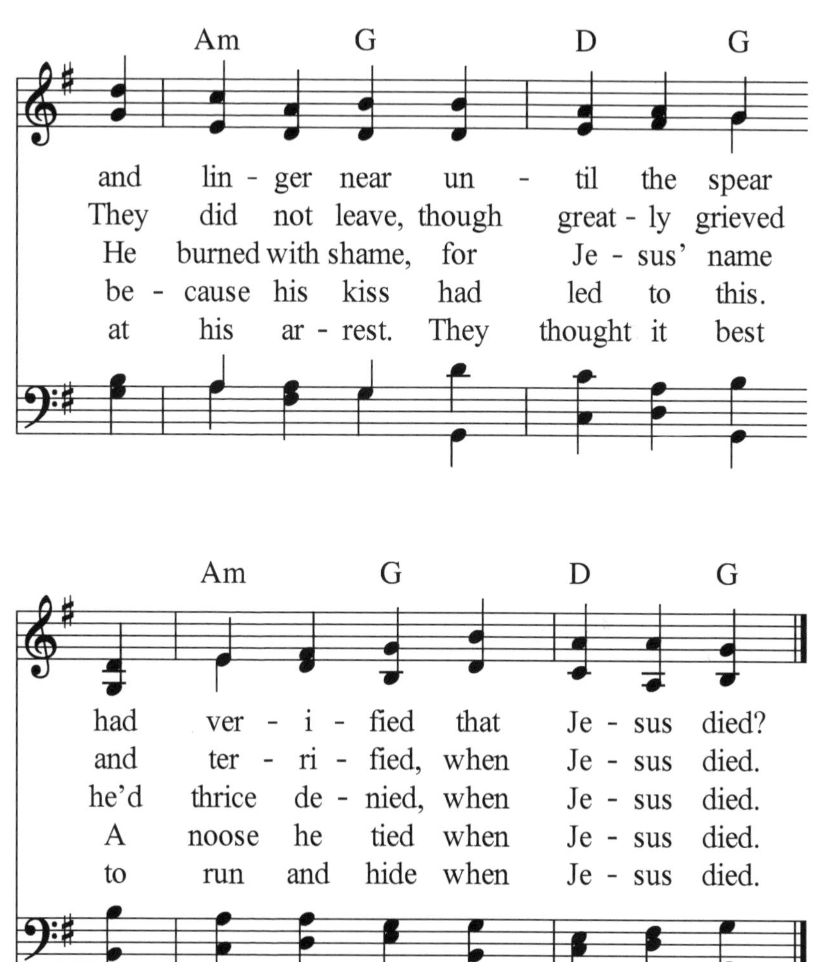
Am G D G
and lin - ger near un - til the spear
They did not leave, though great - ly grieved
He burned with shame, for Je - sus' name
be - cause his kiss had led to this.
at his ar - rest. They thought it best
Am G D G
had ver - i - fied that Je - sus died?
and ter - ri - fied, when Je - sus died.
he'd thrice de - nied, when Je - sus died.
A noose he tied when Je - sus died.
to run and hide when Je - sus died.

O My God, Please Tell Me Why

Linda Bonney Olin, 2016 — George J. Elvey, 1858
(ST. GEORGE'S WINDSOR; alt. harm.)

MAGDALENE sings the melody line. MOTHER sings the alto line.

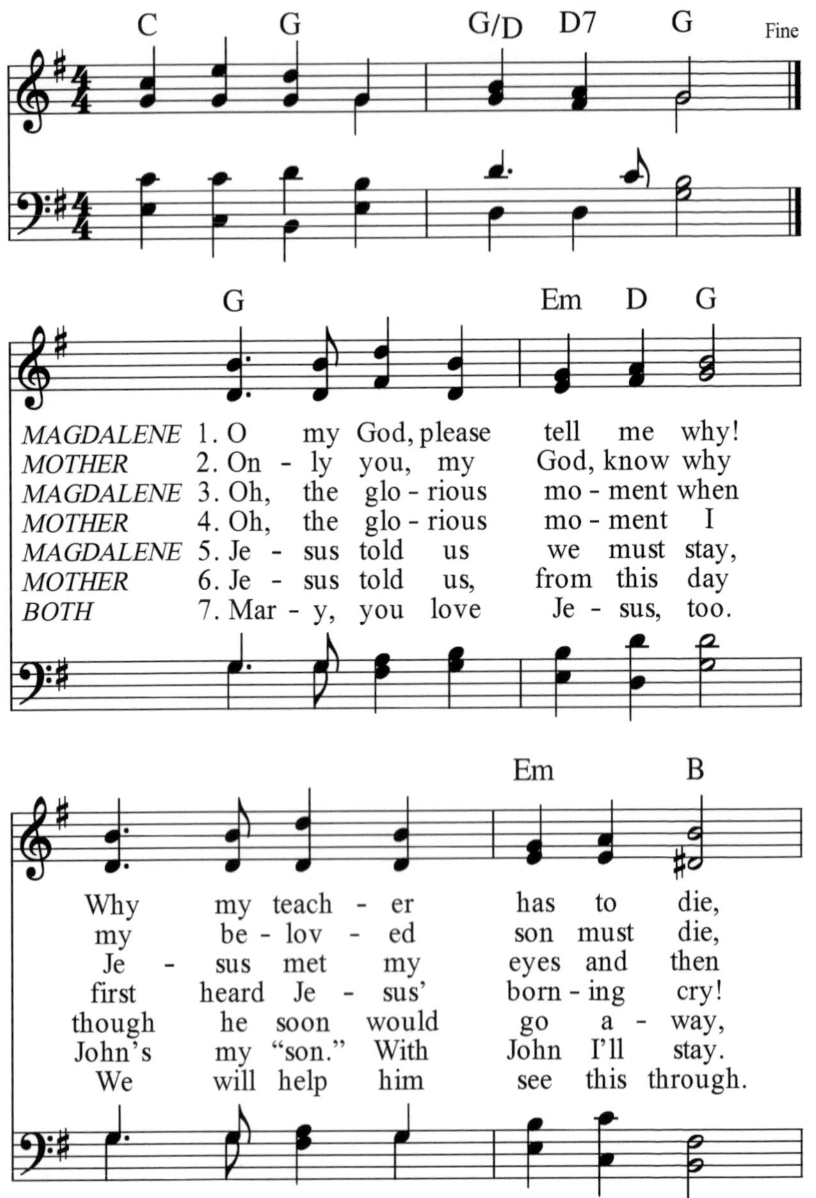
C G G/D D7 G
Fine
G Em D G
MAGDALENE 1. O my God, please tell me why!
MOTHER 2. On - ly you, my God, know why
MAGDALENE 3. Oh, the glo - rious mo - ment when
MOTHER 4. Oh, the glo - rious mo - ment I
MAGDALENE 5. Je - sus told us we must stay,
MOTHER 6. Je - sus told us, from this day
BOTH 7. Mar - y, you love Je - sus, too.
Em B
Why my teach - er has to die,
my be - lov - ed son must die,
Je - sus met my eyes and then
first heard Je - sus' born - ing cry!
though he soon would go a - way,
John's my "son." With John I'll stay.
We will help him see this through.

O MY GOD, PLEASE TELL ME WHY

O MY GOD, PLEASE TELL ME WHY

We're skipping a page to keep the following scores on facing pages. Feel free to scribble notes here.

Jesus, Please Remember Me (Piano)

Linda Bonney Olin, 2016 — William B. Bradbury, 1863
(SOLID ROCK, alt.)

1. I do be - lieve that you are he
2. For all my crimes, I know that I
3. What strange com - pas - sion you have shown,

whom proph - ets called the Prom - ised One.
de - serve this cross of pain and shame.
to say we'll meet in par - a - dise!

Though "King of Jews" the mock - ers see,
But you were whipped and made to die,
I hear a cry... a dy - ing groan...

you're tru - ly King of eve - ry - one.
though in - no - cent of an - y blame.
So, fin - ished is your sac - ri - fice.

JESUS, PLEASE REMEMBER ME (PIANO)

And when your king - dom comes to be,
Your name will soon be praised on high.
Now, Je - sus, are you on your throne?

then, Je - sus, please re - mem - ber me.
Then, Je - sus, don't for - get my cry.
Then num - ber me a - mong your own.

1, 2

O Je - sus, please re - mem - ber me!
O Je - sus, don't for - get my cry!
Oh, num - ber me a - mong your own!

3

I trust in you to set me free. Have mer - cy,

and re - mem - ber me! O Je - sus, please re - mem - ber me!

Jesus, Please Remember Me (Chords)

Linda Bonney Olin, 2016 — William B. Bradbury, 1863
(SOLID ROCK, alt.)

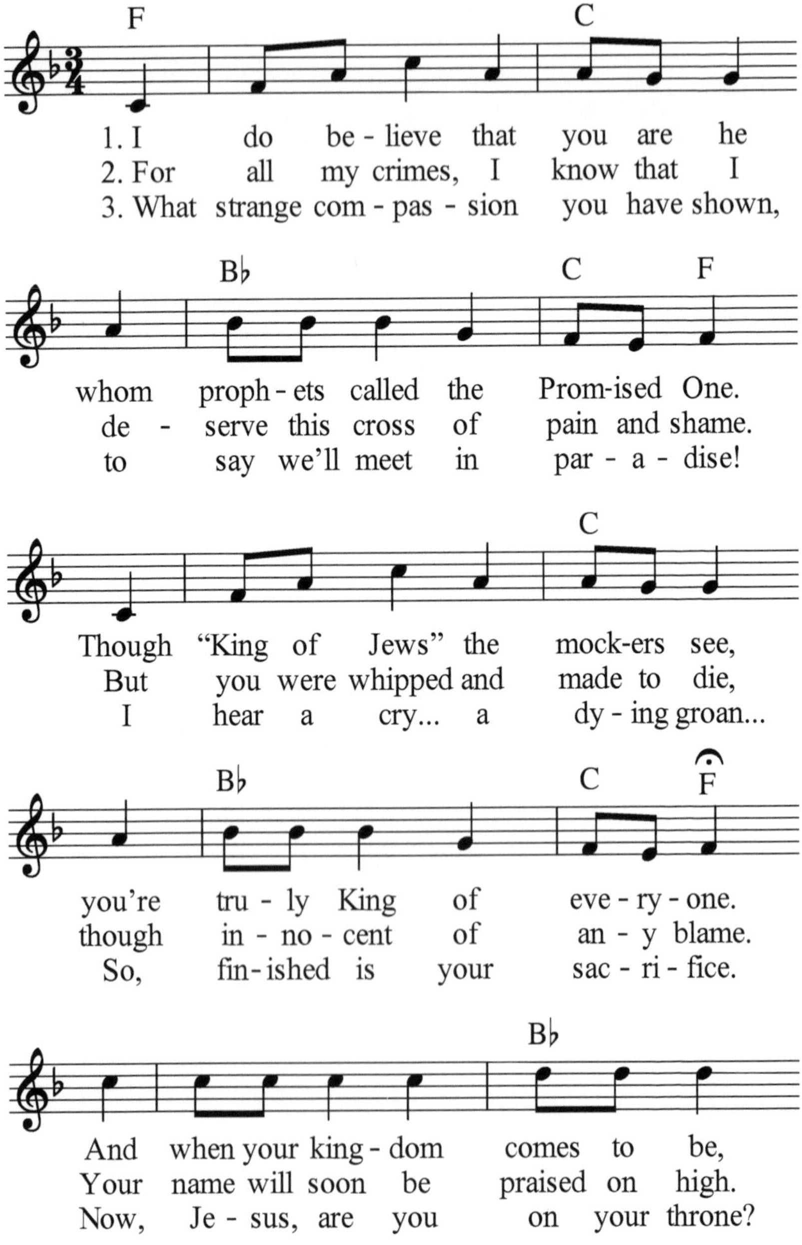

F C

1. I do be - lieve that you are he
2. For all my crimes, I know that I
3. What strange com - pas - sion you have shown,

B♭ C F

whom proph - ets called the Prom-ised One.
de - serve this cross of pain and shame.
to say we'll meet in par - a - dise!

C

Though "King of Jews" the mock-ers see,
But you were whipped and made to die,
I hear a cry... a dy - ing groan...

B♭ C F

you're tru - ly King of eve - ry - one.
though in - no - cent of an - y blame.
So, fin-ished is your sac - ri - fice.

B♭

And when your king - dom comes to be,
Your name will soon be praised on high.
Now, Je - sus, are you on your throne?

F
C
then, Je - sus, please re - mem - ber me.
Then, Je - sus, don't for - get my cry.
Then num - ber me a - mong your own.
F Bb F C7 F
1, 2
O Je - sus, please re - mem - ber me!
O Je - sus, don't for - get my cry!
Oh, num - ber me a - mong your own!
3
Bb
I trust in you to set me free.
F
C
Have mer - cy, and re - mem - ber me!
F Bb F C7 F
O Je - sus, please re - mem - ber me!

My God, Why

Linda Bonney Olin, 2016

John Dowland, 1603
(Time Stands Still)
Arr. Linda Bonney Olin, 2016

𝅗𝅥 = 70

Oboe Intro/ Solo Voice

Bass Viol

6

1. "My God, why?" re - sounds on
2. One last cry, ex - claim - ing,
3. Dark noon sky. Earth quakes. Cre -
4. Tear - swelled eyes in dawn - ing

8

Cal - va - ry, where now the
"It___ is done!" Tri - um - phant
a - tion knows! The tem - ple
light___ be - hold an emp - ty

10

man called___ Je - sus,___ King of the Jews, hangs
words! His spir - it___ he will soon yield to
veil from___ top to___ bot - tom is torn as
grave! Re - joice! He___ once a - gain lives who

12
cru - ci - fied. "My God, my God, oh why
hands a - bove. Al - might - y God on high,
Je - sus dies. When sol - diers pierce his side,
had been slain! Death's pow'r the Christ de - fies.
15
have you for - sak - en me?"
well pleased, a - waits his Son.
blood mixed with wa - ter flows.
He keeps God's word of old,
17
Not one com - mand did Je - sus re -
Je - sus en - dures his fi - nal or -
On - look - ers wail and fol - low - ers
sin - ners to save. New life Je - sus
19
fuse. Why now does the face of God hide?
deal in per - fect, o - be - di - ent love.
mourn when cold in a tomb Je - sus lies.
gives, in glo - ry for - ev - er to reign!

Where Are You, My God

Linda Bonney Olin, 2014 — Philip P. Bliss, 1875
(LIGHT OF THE WORLD, alt.)

1. Where are you, my God? How I
2. Where are you, my God? How I
3. Where are you, my God? Do you

need you to-day! Oh, touch me, this ver-y hour!_
want you to say, "I'm with you, this ver-y min - ute!"
still hear me pray? Please an - swer, this ver-y sec - ond!

Your pres - ence would mean more than
I'm search - ing the cloud that turned
I'm try - ing, dear Fa - ther, your

an - y dis-play of heav-en's ma - jes - tic pow - er.
blue sky to gray but don't see your face with - in it.
will to o - bey. It's hard - er than I had reck-oned.

Refrain
I miss you so! Why don't you feel near?
Where did it go, your voice in my ear?
Help me to know you tru - ly are here,
and stay, come what may to - mor - row.

Roll the Stone Away

Linda Bonney Olin, 2017
Arthur S. Sullivan, 1871
(ST. GERTRUDE)
♩ = 120
1. Je - sus, with the dawn - ing,
2. Roll a - way the cur - tain
3. Roll a - way the trac - es
4. Roll a - way our ques - tions,
roll a - way our gloom, for your dy - ing
from our point of view. O - pen up our
of our par - doned sin. Clear the way for
eve - ry lin - g'ring doubt. Let the light of
ends in vic - to - ry, not doom.
eyes to what God's pow'r can do.
grace and love to grow with - in.
truth in. Chase the dark - ness out.
There's no need for tears or
With the ris - ing sun, we
Seek - ing to be ho - ly,
Hear more voic - es join - ing,

bur - i - al per - fume. When the stone is
see you ris - en too. When the stone is
claim - ing Christ as kin, when the stone is
ea - ger and de - vout. When the stone is
rolled a - way, there stands an emp - ty tomb.
rolled a - way, we find the liv - ing you!
rolled a - way, new life we shall be - gin.
rolled a - way, we'll raise a joy - ful shout!
Show the world to - day, O Lord!
Show the world to - day! Show your ris - en
glo - ry! Roll the stone a - way!

We Were All There

Linda Bonney Olin, 2016;
adapted from "Were You There"

African-American spiritual

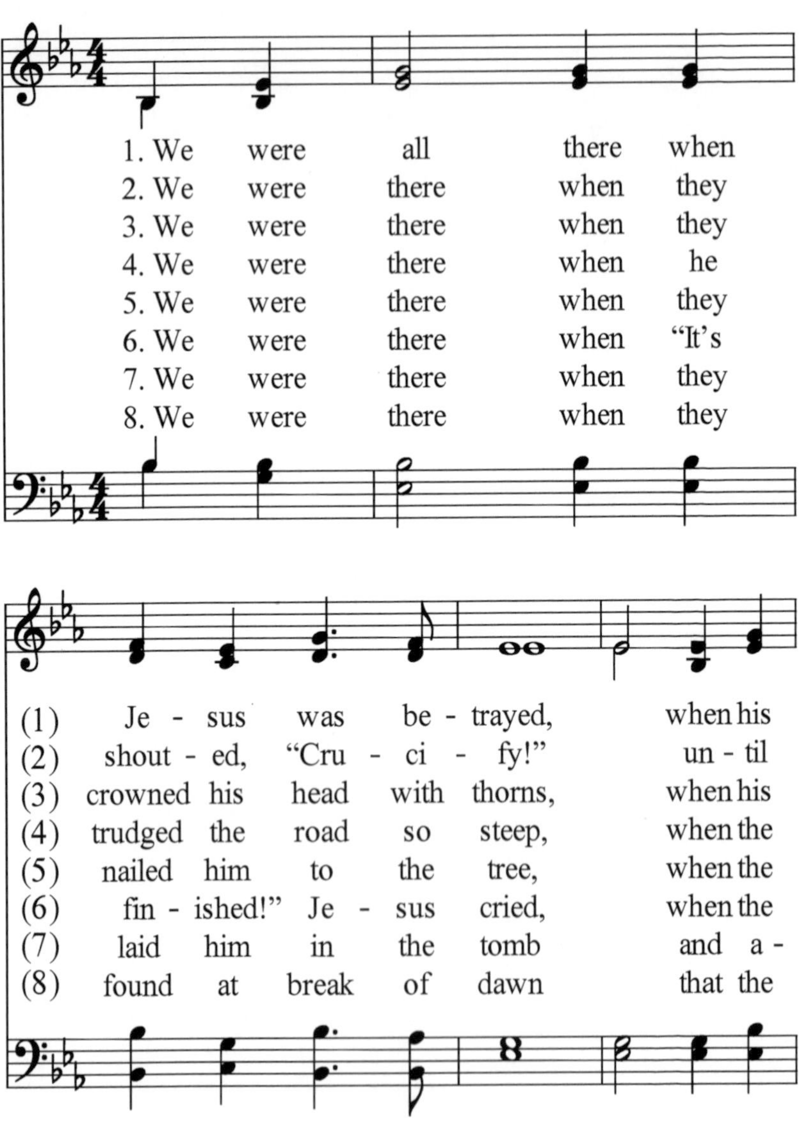
1. We were all there when
2. We were there when they
3. We were there when they
4. We were there when he
5. We were there when they
6. We were there when "It's
7. We were there when they
8. We were there when they
(1) Je - sus was be - trayed, when his
(2) shout - ed, "Cru - ci - fy!" un - til
(3) crowned his head with thorns, when his
(4) trudged the road so steep, when the
(5) nailed him to the tree, when the
(6) fin - ished!" Je - sus cried, when the
(7) laid him in the tomb and a -
(8) found at break of dawn that the

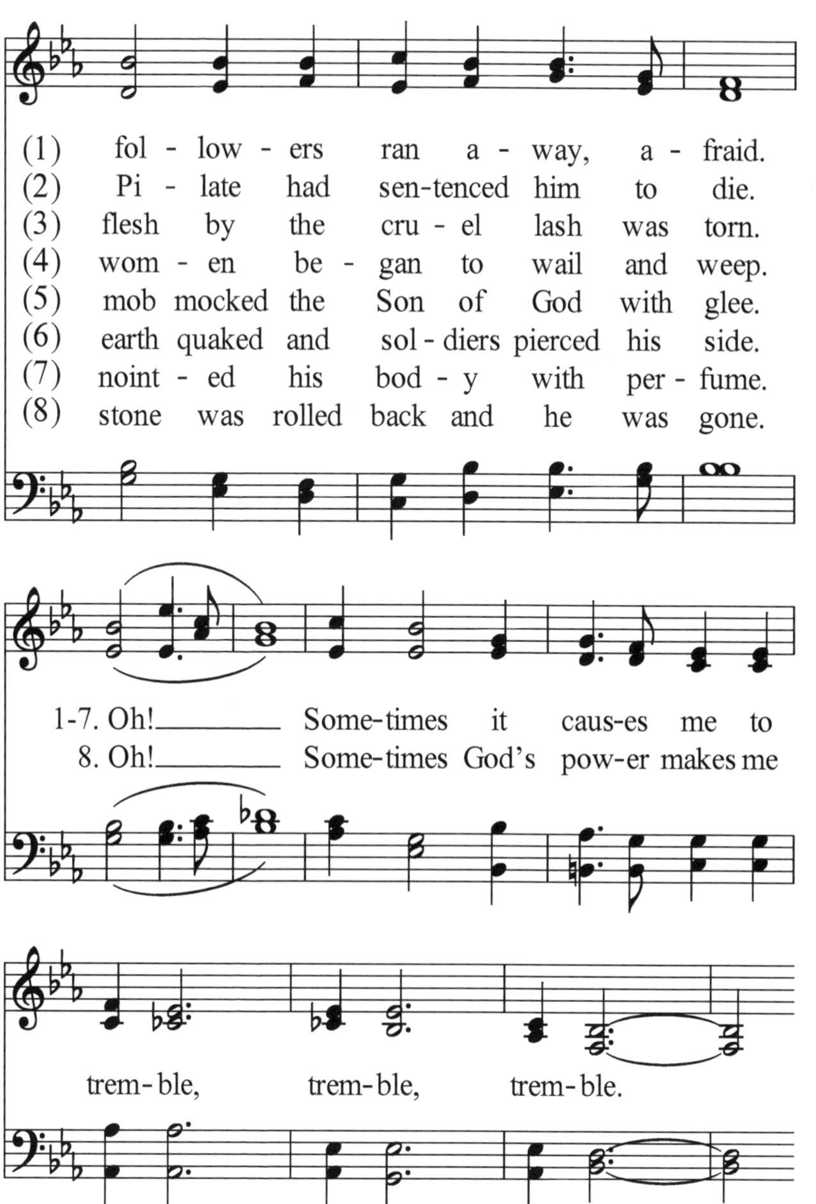
(1) fol - low - ers ran a - way, a - fraid.
(2) Pi - late had sen-tenced him to die.
(3) flesh by the cru - el lash was torn.
(4) wom - en be - gan to wail and weep.
(5) mob mocked the Son of God with glee.
(6) earth quaked and sol - diers pierced his side.
(7) noint - ed his bod - y with per - fume.
(8) stone was rolled back and he was gone.
1-7. Oh! Some-times it caus-es me to
8. Oh! Some-times God's pow-er makes me
trem- ble, trem- ble, trem- ble.

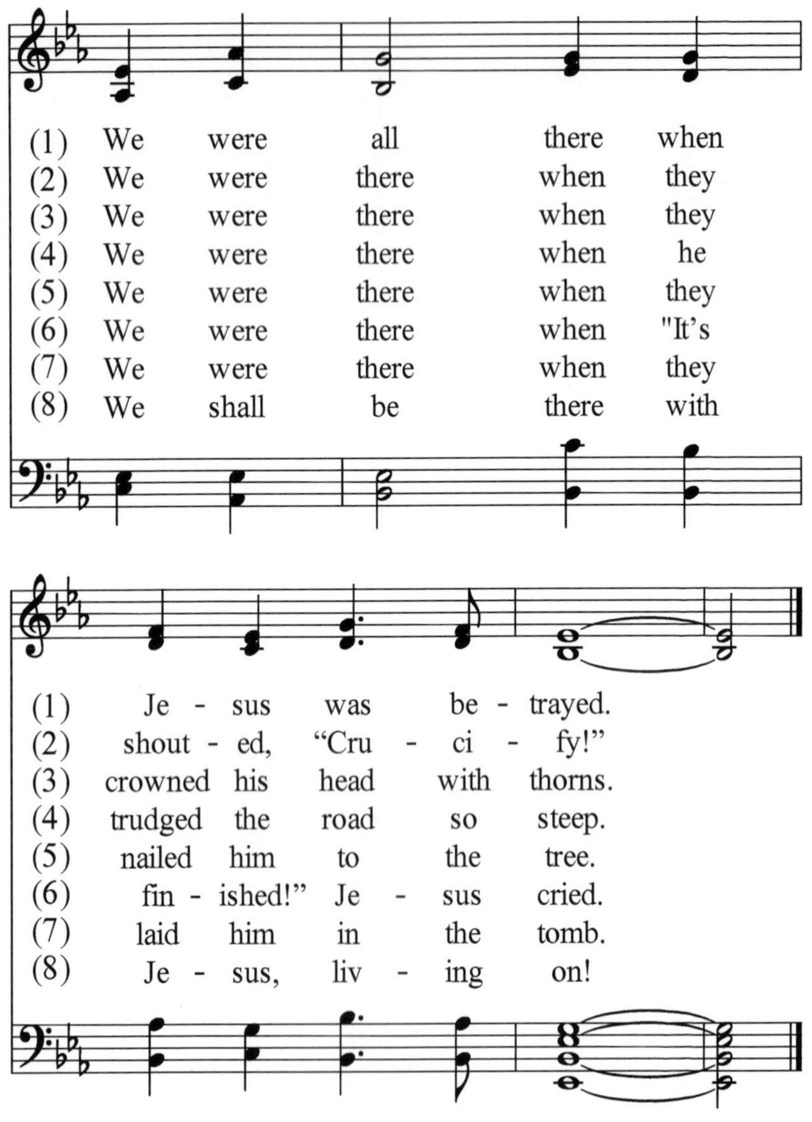
(1) We were all there when
(2) We were there when they
(3) We were there when they
(4) We were there when he
(5) We were there when they
(6) We were there when "It's
(7) We were there when they
(8) We shall be there with
(1) Je - sus was be - trayed.
(2) shout - ed, "Cru - ci - fy!"
(3) crowned his head with thorns.
(4) trudged the road so steep.
(5) nailed him to the tree.
(6) fin - ished!" Je - sus cried.
(7) laid him in the tomb.
(8) Je - sus, liv - ing on!

SONG TEXTS

Jesus, Please Remember Me

1. I do believe that you are he
whom prophets called the Promised One.
Though "King of Jews" the mockers see,
you're truly King of everyone.
And when your kingdom comes to be,
then, Jesus, please remember me.
O Jesus, please remember me!

2. For all my crimes, I know that I
deserve this cross of pain and shame.
But you were whipped and made to die,
though innocent of any blame.
Your name will soon be praised on high.
Then, Jesus, don't forget my cry.
O Jesus, don't forget my cry!

3. What strange compassion you have shown,
to say we'll meet in paradise!
I hear a cry . . . a dying groan . . .
So, finished is your sacrifice.
Now, Jesus, are you on your throne?
Then number me among your own.
Oh, number me among your own!
I trust in you to set me free.
Have mercy, and remember me.
O Jesus, please remember me!

My God, Why

1. “My God, why?”
resounds on Calvary,
where now the man
called Jesus, King of the Jews,
hangs crucified.

“My God, my God, oh why
have you forsaken me?”
Not one command
did Jesus refuse.
Why now does the face of God hide?

2. One last cry,
exclaiming, “It is done!”
Triumphant words!
His spirit he will soon yield
to hands above.

Almighty God on high,
well pleased, awaits his Son.
Jesus endures
his final ordeal
in perfect, obedient love.

3. Dark noon sky.
Earth quakes. Creation knows!
The temple veil
from top to bottom is torn
as Jesus dies.

When soldiers pierce his side,
blood mixed with water flows.
Onlookers wail
and followers mourn
when cold in a tomb Jesus lies.

4. Tear-swelled eyes
in dawning light behold
an empty grave!
Rejoice! He once again lives
who had been slain!

Death's pow'r the Christ defies.
He keeps God's word of old,
sinners to save.
New life Jesus gives,
in glory forever to reign!

O My God, Please Tell Me Why

1. *(Magdalene)* O my God, please tell me why!
Why my teacher has to die,
why such suff'ring you demand
of this gentle, godly man.
Has he broken any law?
Have you found in him some flaw?
Why this cruel death and shame,
when he's innocent of blame?

2. *(Mother)* Only you, my God, know why
my beloved son must die,
how his suff'ring fits your plan:
save the world through God Made Man.
Though it's we who broke your law,
he without a single flaw,
innocent of any blame,
hangs upon a cross of shame.

3. *(Magdalene)* Oh, the glorious moment when
Jesus met my eyes and then
cast my seven demons out!
He's what love is all about!
God, I fear my heart will break
if my teacher's life you take.
You ask more than I can give.
Without him, how can I live?

4. *(Mother)* Oh, the glorious moment I
first heard Jesus' borning cry!
How could there be any doubt?
He's your promise carried out!

Yes, I know my heart will break
when my son— your Son— you take.
Yet, because his life he'll give,
sinners may forever live.

5. *(Magdalene)* Jesus told us we must stay,
though he soon would go away,
leaving even me behind.
Was it death he had in mind?
Soon I'll lose my dearest friend
and our kingdom hopes will end.
But till then, I need to be
strong, as long as he needs me.

6. *(Mother)* Jesus told us, from this day
John's my "son." With John I'll stay.
Even now, on Jesus' mind,
not his own concerns but mine!
Soon his earthly life will end.
Heaven's throne he will ascend.
But for now, he needs from me
comfort in his agony.

7. *(Both)* Mary, you love Jesus, too.
We will help him see this through.
Come and hold my trembling hand
while beneath his cross we stand.
One who watches from above
has an even greater love.
God, give Jesus strength this day.
Fill us with your peace, we pray.

Roll the Stone Away

1. Jesus, with the dawning, roll away our gloom,
for your dying ends in triumph, not in doom.
There's no need for tears or burial perfume.
When the stone is rolled away,
there stands an empty tomb!

Show the world today, O Lord!
Show the world today!
Show your risen glory! Roll the stone away!

2. Roll away the curtain from our point of view.
Open up our eyes to what God's pow'r can do.
With the rising sun, we see you risen too.
When the stone is rolled away,
we find the living you!

Show the world today, O Lord!
Show the world today!
Show your risen glory! Roll the stone away!

3. Roll away the traces of our pardoned sin.
Clear the way for grace and love to grow within.
Seeking to be holy, claiming Christ as kin,
when the stone is rolled away,
new life we shall begin.

Show the world today, O Lord!
Show the world today!
Show your risen glory! Roll the stone away!

4. Roll away our questions, every ling'ring doubt.
Let the light of truth in. Chase the darkness out.
Hear more voices joining, eager and devout.
When the stone is rolled away,
we'll raise a joyful shout!

Show the world today, O Lord!
Show the world today!
Show your risen glory! Roll the stone away!

God Be with You till We Meet Again

God be with you till we meet again;
by his counsels guide, uphold you,
with his sheep securely fold you;
God be with you till we meet again.

Till we meet, till we meet,
till we meet at Jesus' feet;
till we meet, till we meet,
God be with you till we meet again.

We Were All There

1. We were all there when Jesus was betrayed,
when his followers ran away, afraid. Oh!
Sometimes it causes me to tremble, tremble, tremble.
We were all there when Jesus was betrayed.

2. We were there when they shouted, "Crucify!"
until Pilate had sentenced him to die. Oh!
Sometimes it causes me to tremble, tremble, tremble.
We were there when they shouted, "Crucify!"

3. We were there when they crowned his head with thorn,
when his flesh by the cruel lash was torn. Oh!
Sometimes it causes me to tremble, tremble, tremble.
We were there when they crowned his head with thorn.

4. We were there when he trudged the road so steep,
when the women began to wail and weep. Oh!
Sometimes it causes me to tremble, tremble, tremble.
We were there when he trudged the road so steep.

5. We were there when they nailed him to the tree,
when the mob mocked the Son of God with glee. Oh!
Sometimes it causes me to tremble, tremble, tremble.
We were there when they nailed him to the tree.

6. We were there when “It’s finished!” Jesus cried,
when the earth quaked and soldiers pierced his side. Oh!
Sometimes it causes me to tremble, tremble, tremble.
We were there when "It’s finished!” Jesus cried.

7. We were there when they laid him in the tomb
and anointed his body with perfume. Oh!
Sometimes it causes me to tremble, tremble, tremble.
We were there when they laid him in the tomb.

8. We were there when they found at break of dawn
that the stone was rolled back and he was gone. Oh!
Sometimes God’s power makes me tremble, tremble,
tremble.
We shall be there with Jesus, living on!

Were You There

1. Were you there when they crucified my Lord?
Were you there when they crucified my Lord? Oh!
Sometimes it causes me to tremble, tremble, tremble.
Were you there when they crucified my Lord?

2. Were you there when the sun refused to shine?
Were you there when the sun refused to shine? Oh!
Sometimes it causes me to tremble, tremble, tremble.
Were you there when the sun refused to shine?

3. Were you there when they pierced him in the side?
Were you there when they pierced him in the side? Oh!
Sometimes it causes me to tremble, tremble, tremble.
Were you there when they pierced him in the side?

4. Were you there when his friends all ran away?
Were you there when his friends all ran away? Oh!
Sometimes it causes me to tremble, tremble, tremble.
Were you there when his friends all ran away?

5. Were you there when they nailed him to the tree?
Were you there when they nailed him to the tree? Oh!
Sometimes it causes me to tremble, tremble, tremble.
Were you there when they nailed him to the tree?

6. Were you there when they crucified my Lord?
Were you there when they crucified my Lord? Oh!
Sometimes it causes me to tremble, tremble, tremble.
Were you there when they crucified my Lord?

7. Were you there when the women wept and wailed?
Were you there when the women wept and wailed? Oh!
Sometimes it causes me to tremble, tremble, tremble.
Were you there when the women wept and wailed?

8. Were you there when they mocked the Son of God?
Were you there when they mocked the Son of God? Oh!
Sometimes it causes me to tremble, tremble, tremble.
Were you there when they mocked the Son of God?

9. Were you there when the thief called Jesus "King"?
Were you there when the thief called Jesus "King"? Oh!
Sometimes it causes me to tremble, tremble, tremble.
Were you there when the thief called Jesus "King"?

10. Were you there when he cried, "My God, my God"?
Were you there when he cried, "My God, my God"? Oh!
Sometimes it causes me to tremble, tremble, tremble.
Were you there when he cried, "My God, my God"?

11. Were you there when the earth began to quake?
Were you there when the earth began to quake? Oh!
Sometimes it causes me to tremble, tremble, tremble.
Were you there when the earth began to quake?

Who Is This Man

1. I was there the day that Jesus died.
I will simply tell what I saw.
All of you, when I have testified,
may your own conclusions draw.
You should know that I did not merely see
what transpired on Golgotha hill.
It was my own hand that nailed him to the tree,
and that knowledge haunts me still.

2. I'm a Roman soldier. I obey
without question every command.
And the order Pilate gave that day
was to crucify a man.
Yes, a Jew named Jesus the Nazarene
was condemned on the cross to die.
I inscribed the charges to be plainly seen:
"King of Jews." I'll tell you why.

3. The religious leaders had accused
him of stirring up a revolt,
as the Son of God and King of Jews,
titles only Caesar could hold.
So we mocked this "king" with a royal cloak,
crown of thorns stabbed into his head,
and I scourged his back with such a vicious stroke
that it hung in bloody shreds.

4. Did that bother me? No, not at all.
I had scourged men hundreds of times.
That's the price, by Roman protocol,
convicts pay for terrible crimes.
We made Jesus shoulder a heavy beam.
To Golgotha he bore its weight.
There he fell and stretched his arms so wide, it seemed
he embraced his coming fate.

5. When I pressed his hands against the wood
and began to hammer the spikes,
far from cursing me, as some men would,
he looked deep into my eyes.
"Father, please forgive them for what they do,
for they don't understand," he cried.
I just pounded harder, for I thought I knew
he was justly crucified.

6. When we hoisted Jesus' cross in place,
every nail ripped through his flesh more.
There he hung in torment and disgrace,
but such things I'd learned to ignore.
Having stripped our prisoners' clothing off,
we divided the goods we'd seized.
But for Jesus' tunic we instead cast lots,
for it was one seamless piece.

7. Nine o'clock: Three crucifixions done,
Jesus plus two dangerous thieves.
We four soldiers, the centurion,
and the jeering crowd were pleased.

Hecklers called, “Hail, King of the Jews!” with glee.
“Save yourself, Son of God Most High!”
“Yes, Messiah! Save yourself, and then save me,”
mocked a thief who hung at his side.

8. But the second thief rebuked the first.
“Don’t you fear God’s punishment?
We are guilty and deserve the worst,
but this man is innocent.”
Then he said to Jesus, “Remember me
in your kingdom,” to my surprise.
Jesus answered, “Truly I say you will meet
me today in paradise!”

9. Jesus, innocent? He’d had a trial.
Pilate must have had a good cause.
But there happened, in a little while,
strange events that gave me pause.
Close to noon the sky began turning black,
though I’d not seen a single cloud.
Lightning flashed above us, and the thunder cracked.
Three o’clock: Jesus cried out loud.

10. “Oh, my God,” with passion Jesus prayed.
“Why have you forsaken me?”
Could a guilty dying man have made
such a fervent, anguished plea?
Someone offered Jesus some sour wine.
Then his voice once again rang out,
saying, “It is finished!” For the final time,
Jesus’ thorn-crowned head he bowed.

11. All at once, I felt Golgotha shake.
Boulders split and crashed on the ground.
People trying to escape the quake
in a panic stumbled around.
Though a soldier always must be prepared,
by this pow'r we were overawed.
The centurion, upon his knees, declared,
"Truly, he was the Son of God!"

12. When the rocking earth grew calm, I found
both the robbers still were alive.
They must die before the sun went down
and the Jewish Sabbath arrived.
So we broke their legs, that the end be rushed;
but for Jesus I raised my spear.
When I pierced his side, both blood and water gushed.
He was dead. That was very clear.

13. Two men, bringing ointments and perfume,
took the body down from the cross.
Then they placed it in a nearby tomb,
and we rolled a stone across.
Soon the sun went down and the day was done,
but I still didn't understand.
Were we soldiers standing watch on God's own son?
Who was— Who *is* this man?
Were we soldiers standing watch on God's own son?
Who was— Who *is* this man?

Where Are You, My God

1. Where are you, my God? How I need you today!
Oh, touch me, this very hour!
Your presence would mean more than any display
of heaven's majestic power.

I miss you so! Why don't you feel near?
Where did it go, your voice in my ear?
Help me to know you truly are here,
and stay, come what may tomorrow.

2. Where are you, my God? How I want you to say,
"I'm with you, this very minute!"
I'm searching the cloud that turned blue sky to gray
but don't see your face within it.

I miss you so! Why don't you feel near?
Where did it go, your voice in my ear?
Help me to know you truly are here,
and stay, come what may tomorrow.

3. Where are you, my God? Do you still hear me pray?
Please answer, this very second!
I'm trying, dear Father, your will to obey.
It's harder than I had reckoned.

I miss you so! Why don't you feel near?
Where did it go, your voice in my ear?
Help me to know you truly are here,
and stay, come what may tomorrow.

Where Were the Twelve

1. Where were the twelve when Jesus died?
Did his disciples stand at Jesus' side
and linger near until the spear
had verified that Jesus died?

2. Yes, John was there when Jesus died.
John and the women saw him crucified.
They did not leave, though greatly grieved
and terrified, when Jesus died.

3. Was Peter there when Jesus died?
No, Simon Peter sat alone and cried.
He burned with shame, for Jesus' name
he'd thrice denied, when Jesus died.

4. Was Judas there, when Jesus died?
No, the betrayer, torn by guilt inside
because his kiss had come to this,
a noose had tied when Jesus died.

5. Where were the rest when Jesus died?
All of them scattered, as he'd prophesied.
At his arrest, they thought it best
to run and hide when Jesus died.

ABOUT THE AUTHOR

Linda Bonney Olin is a veteran leader of Bible studies and Sunday school programs for adults. She was certified as a lay speaker in the United Methodist Church in 1997. Her writing ministry has produced a wealth of dramas, songs, sermons, puppet plays, and special programs for interdenominational church groups. Her poems, devotions, short fiction, hymns, and Bible study materials have been published in literary and devotional magazines, anthologies, hymnals, and online publications.

Visit www.LindaBonneyOlin.com to contact Linda, learn more about her and her work, and find a variety of resources for ministry, music, and writing. Check the Audio page to listen to examples of the music from this book and Linda's other songs and hymns. Performances of selected songs may be heard on her YouTube channel.

ALSO BY LINDA BONNEY OLIN

Now Sings My Soul

New Songs for the Lord

More than a hundred hymns and faith songs with lyrics by Linda Bonney Olin, presented in stanza format for easy reading and also in musical settings. Some feature original music; most are set to classic hymn tunes. Includes indexes of relevant scripture passages and suggested themes/occasions for use in worship.

Songs for the Lord

A Book of Twenty-Four Original Hymns and Faith Songs

A mix of congregational hymns, soulful solos, hand-clapping gospel, and humorous songs. Lyrics and melodies; no piano accompaniment. (Updated versions of some songs from this collection appear with full accompaniment in *Now Sings My Soul.*)

Transformed

5 Resurrection Dramas

Five one-act plays to read or perform with a small cast. Each play explores how a person close to Jesus was transformed by his resurrection:

- Simon Peter (dramatic comedy)
- John the Apostle (dramatic monologue)
- James the Brother of Jesus (dramatic comedy with five short ensemble songs; plus an alternate interview version)
- Mary the Mother of Jesus (light drama)
- Mary Magdalene (dramatic monologue with optional solo songs)

The Sacrifice Support Group

A Dramatic Comedy for Lent

Laugh and learn along with a mixed bag of church characters challenged by their pastor to make Lenten sacrifices that glorify God and benefit their families and community—even the world!

Two twenty-minute acts. Cast: 1 M, 3 F; 3 M/F. Ideal for actors with limited mobility. Virtually no staging required. Easy to put on as Readers Theatre with little or no preparation.

Giving It Up for Lent—Leader Guide

Bible Study, Drama, Discussion

Complete guide to leading a fun, life-changing, five-to-seven session study of Lenten sacrifice, featuring *The Sacrifice Support Group*. Includes an introductory look at Bible accounts of people who offered sacrifices to the Lord; in-depth discussion questions; and the drama script. For adults and older teens.

Giving It Up for Lent—Workbook

Bible Study, Drama, Discussion

Optional individual book for study participants. Includes *The Sacrifice Support Group* script plus workbook pages corresponding to the Bible passages and discussion questions in the leader guide.

Printed in Great Britain
by Amazon

36050323R00075